SAFETY AND HEALTH AT SEA

by Arne Sagen, MNI, ALCM/USA
and
Pat Mitchell, BA, BAI

A Practical Manual for Seafarers

DNV

SAFETY AND HEALTH AT SEA

WITHERBY

PUBLISHERS

First Published 2002
© Arne Sagen and Pat Mitchell

PUBLISHERS AND SOLE DISTRIBUTORS

Witherby & Company Limited
32–36 Aylesbury Street
London EC1R 0ET
Tel. No: +44 20 7251 5341
Fax. No: +44 20 7251 1296
Website: www.witherbys.com
Email: books@witherbys.co.uk

Anne Sagen, Pat Mitchell
ISBN 1 85609 233 X

Printed in London by
Witherby & Company Limited

British Library Cataloguing in Publication Data
Sagen, Arne and Mitchell, Pat
Safety and Health at Sea
I. Title
ISBN 1 85609 233 X

Cover photograph by courtesy of Videotel Marine International

PREFACE

The safety and health of seafarers is protected by an impressive framework of conventions and legislation. The IMO's International Safety Management Code, the ILO's Maritime conventions, European Union Directives for Safety and Health at Work and the legislation of maritime nations together set the standards for creating a safe and healthy working environment at sea.

The purpose of this manual is to highlight the basic principles which the framework contains and help seafarers put them into practice.

We have described how to implement the procedures, such as risk assessment and safety inspections, which can prevent accidents. We have provided guidance on how to maintain high levels of health and hygiene on board. We have included checklists to help seafarers focus on the hazards of particular operations on their ships. And we have suggested how an understanding of the human factor in accident prevention can be used to create a strong and resilient safety culture on board.

Safe and healthy working practices benefit everyone from individual seafarers to the companies they work for and the customers who rely on the services those companies provide.

We hope that seafarers will find this manual useful in their efforts to maintain and strengthen *Safety and Health at Sea.*

Arne Sagen	Pat Mitchell	August 2002
Oslo	Cambridge	
Norway	England	

THE AUTHORS

Arne Sagen (MNIF, ALCM, CNI) has a multidisciplinary experience from ship operation ranging from seafarer, shipping companies superintendent, engineering chief, chief research engineer, manager of the shipping research program "Ship Operation of the Future", and DNV principal surveyor.

He is authorized as ISO 9000 quality assessor, ISM Code lead auditor, appointed flag state inspector for Namibia and port state inspector for Egypt and Trinidad and Tobago and appointed quality assessor by IACS (International Association of Classification Societies, UK).

He has a US degree qualifying as an Industrial Hygienist.

He is author of several textbooks within areas of ship operation such as auxiliary power plants, maritime satellite communication, computer supported ship operation, the ISM Code in practice etc.

Pat Mitchell began his career as a Production Engineer, working in manufacturing operations in marine engine building, mechanical and electronic engineering in Europe and North America. For the past thirty years he has been a consultant and writer specialising in management training and development.

Amongst his many publications, he has written guides for Videotel International Limited, who provide multi-media training programmes for the world-wide shipping industry. These include a comprehensive, CD-ROM based programme for training ships' Safety Officers, guides to the *Management for Seafarers* video series, and other video based programmes such as *Marine Risk Assessment* and *Personal Survival at Sea SOLAS Chapter III*.

ACKNOWLEDGEMENTS

The authors are grateful to a number of people and organisations in the shipping world for supporting and encouraging the writing of this book. We have had the privilege of standing on the shoulders of many distinguished authors, researchers, professional seafarers and organisations active in the improvement of safety, health and the working environment at sea. We are particularly grateful for the help provided by:

Det Norske Veritas for their invaluable encouragement to turn this work from vision to reality. It has been very important to the authors to have the support of a classification society with an internationally recognised role in the certification of the ISM Code. Their support has helped us to focus on the ISM Code's objective to 'provide for safe practices in ship operation and a safe working environment'.

INTERTANKO whose vigorous promotion of the ISM Code Safety Management System as a means of improving safety in shipping helped to reinforce our emphasis on the human factor in the continuous struggle to avoid accidents and injuries at sea.

The Norwegian Non-fiction Literature Fund for enabling international co-operation between non-fiction authors by granting a 'travelling cost' scholarship.

Dr Elif Dahl MD, MHA, PhD (Chair, Section of Cruise Ship and Maritime Medicine and Board Member of The International Maritime Health Association) for verifying and amending Section 3 of the manual, Health on Board, and helping us ensure that the terminology used is acceptable to ships' medical staff and seafarers.

CONTENTS

BIBLIOGRAPHY

In addition to our suggestions for further reading, the authors have included some of the sources which we used for reference when writing this book.

The ISM Code – In practice
by Arne Sagen
publisher Universitetsbiblioteket, Norway
ISBN 82 518 3825 8

Safety and Health Manuals for Seafarers
by Kaare Andre Kopperud and Arne Sagen
publisher Nikas Maritime, Norway
ISBN 82 92093 04 4

Code of Safe Working Practices for Seafarers
publisher United Kingdom Maritime and Coastguard Agency
ISBN 0 11 5518363

Guidelines on the Application of the IMO International Safety Management (ISM) Code
publisher International Chamber of Shipping and International Shipping Federation

Successful Health and Safety Management
publisher United Kingdom Health and Safety Executive
ISBN 0 7176 1276 7

Godt Arbeidmiljø Ombord
publisher by Sjøfarten Arbeidsmiljøråd, Danmark

Report on Protection and Environment Work – Ship and catching vessels, 1994
The Norwegian Maritime Directorate and The Council for Labour Supervision on Norwegian Ships

How to Run a Training Session
by Pat Mitchell
publisher Mitchell Management Training
ISBN 0 9543282 0 5

INTRODUCTION

The Manual

Safety and Health at Sea is a manual designed to help ships' Masters, Safety Supervisors and officers create a safe and healthy working and living environment for all those on board their ships.

There is a large and growing list of conventions, laws and regulations, both national and international, governing safety and health at sea, but the manual is not exclusively about the law. It is about how to put the principles on which the legal framework is based into practice.

The manual is for reference. It is not a book to be read from beginning to end. Use its contents selectively for advice and guidance on particular aspects of safety and health.

The Contents

The manual is divided into six major sections, plus this introduction and a number of appendices. The sections cover:

Section 1:   **Your shipboard safety system**

How to organise safety on board. It is in three sub-sections:

- **Responsibilities.** The Master; the Safety Supervisor; Safety Representatives; the Safety Committee.

- **Structure.** Safety Representatives; Safety Committees; plans and instructions; public display of safety information.

- **Procedures.** Risk Assessment; Safety Inspections; Permit to Work systems; Drills; Accident/Near miss investigation and reporting.

Section 2:   **Tools for improving safety**

Checklists and other types of guidance. In addition to a short introduction, this Section contains:

- **A blank Safety Supervisor's job description**

- **Checklists for safety inspections**

- **Guidance notes for accident prevention**

Section 3:   **Health on board**

Guidance on how to protect seafarers from the principal dangers to their health.

Section 4: **Safety and health training**

Guidance on training for Safety Supervisors, Safety Representatives and other crew members.

Section 5: **Reviewing safety and health on board**

A questionnaire to help the Safety Committee find out what the crew thinks about the status of safety and health on board.

Section 6: **The Human Factor**

- Safety culture: what it is; practical issues for managers and officers.

- Understanding accidents: the Safety Iceberg; the causes of accidents; human behaviour

Appendices: **Relevant IMO, ILO and EU regulations**

- The ISM Code (with items of particular relevance to safety and health on board highlighted in bold).

- The STCW Convention and its relationship to the ISM Code.

- ILO Minimum Standards Convention no. 147 (Enforced by global Port State Control).

- ILO Convention 178 concerning the inspection of seafarers working and living conditions (excerpts)

- Brief summaries and excerpts from relevant EU Council Directives for ships flying EU flags

The Background

"The shipping industry cannot go on in this way, with over 1000 deaths from accidents among seafarers every year" – William O'Neill, Secretary General, The International Maritime Organisation.

Everyone involved in shipping benefits from making the industry safer. Accidents cost money and can result in claims from customers, so shipping companies benefit from their reduction. Improvements to safety benefit customers by reducing the damage and delay which accidents create. And seafarers benefit from being able to earn their livings without suffering the consequences to themselves and their families of being injured or killed.

Accidents – causes and solutions

Accidents don't just happen, they are caused. In the shipping industry the most important basic causes are:

- **An imperfect safety culture at company level**

  Seafarers who can see that safety is not a major priority for their company are unlikely to make it their own.

- **Inadequate safety management**

  Accidents on board are much more likely if policies are unclear, responsibilities are undefined, procedures and controls are absent or only exist on paper and training is inadequate and inappropriate.

- **Individuals with the wrong attitudes to safety**

  Accidents happen when people believe that the rules don't apply to them, that safety is someone else's problem, that their jobs will be easier and quicker if they ignore safe practices or even that working safely is 'soft'.

It is clear from these three major causes where solutions must lie. Companies' safety cultures must be strengthened, effective safety management systems put in place and individuals shown how to change their attitudes and hence their behaviour.

Though that is easier said than done, there are two particular keys to successfully improving safety on board:

- **A realistic action plan, put into practice with energy and enthusiasm**

  Most ships have stacks of rules and regulations governing safety, often written in language which is hard for anyone but lawyers to understand. It is the lack of implementation, not documentation, that is the problem. Seafarers are practical, action oriented people. They will respond to a clear plan of action, particularly one which they can see is being pursued with determination.

- **Recognising the importance of the human factor**

  Rules, procedures, controls and so on, though important, will not improve safety on their own. Major improvements will only come about when each individual puts safety first, both for himself and for his fellow seafarers.

  While this is the case in every industry, it is especially important in shipping. Ships, particularly ocean-going ships, are not like workplaces ashore. They are closed communities of people who live and work together 24 hours a day. Individuals are not subject to the same external influences as those who work ashore, either from senior management when they are at work or from family, friends and so on outside of work. Almost all of the motivation to improve safety therefore has to be generated from within the community of seafarers on each ship.

What level of improvement is possible?

Experience from thousands of shore based companies, and also those in the off-shore industry, demonstrate that:

- The application of a properly designed action plan can reduce accidents by at least 50% over a 3 to 4 year period.

- Improvement need not stop at that point. By updating and implementing the plan again, further reductions of the same order of magnitude can be achieved until accident rates are reduced to a small percentage of their original levels.

That is a goal well worth aiming for in the shipping industry and on every individual ship.

1. YOUR SHIPBOARD SAFETY SYSTEM

1.0 INTRODUCTION

To be effective, safety management on board must be systematic. It must also be continuous. Safety is not a 'problem' which can be solved and then put aside. It is a permanent feature of how everyone on board works and lives.

What this means is that every ship needs a properly functioning system for managing safety. The elements of the system, which are covered in more detail later in this Section, are:

1. **Responsibilities**

    Safety is, of course, everyone's responsibility, but there must be clarity about what that means for specific individuals on board, in particular the Master, the Safety Supervisor, Safety Representatives and the Safety Committee.

2. **Structure**

    Most Flag States and shipping companies require each ship to have a designated Safety Officer, Safety Supervisor and a Safety Committee. The Safety Supervisor may be an officer (as it is on UK flagged ships), but this is not mandatory in all administrations. For example, the Danish, Norwegian and Swedish administrations require the Health and Safety Supervisor to be elected by and from the ratings.

    For the sake of simplicity we will use the term <u>Safety Supervisor</u> in this manual.

    Even if your administration or company does not require you to have a formally designated Safety Supervisor on your ship, it makes sense to identify who is going to handle particular aspects of safety management, including carrying out the procedures described below. [The ISM Code (chapter 3.2) requires the Company to '*define and document the responsibility, authority and interrelation of all personnel who manage, perform and verify work relating to and affecting safety and pollution prevention*].

    Structure also includes having the correct documentation, some of which is required by law.

3. **Procedures**

    Prevention is better than cure, which is why systematic Risk Assessment, regular safety inspections and Permit to Work systems are an essential part of safety management. Of course, emergencies may still occur, so crews must be equipped to handle them by carrying out drills. In addition, accidents and near misses must be properly investigated to prevent them happening again.

The principles of safety management systems, for both shipping companies and individual ships, are established as an international standard in the IMO's International Safety Management (ISM) Code. This Code has been incorporated into the SOLAS (Safety of Life at Sea) Convention. The standard which the Code represents is the basis for the much more detailed laws, regulations and codes of practice of the European Union and individual Flag States.

Note: Most flag state administrations have national regulations covering living and working conditions on board. These often include defined responsibilities, structure and organisation for safety and health. If there should be differences between your national regulations and this manual, the national regulations shall prevail.

1.1 RESPONSIBILITIES

1.1.1 The Master

The Master carries the overall responsibility and authority for safety on board. The ISM Code says:

> *The Company should ensure that the SMS [Safety Management System] operating on board the ship contains a clear statement emphasising the master's authority. The Company should establish in the SMS that the master has the overriding authority and the responsibility to make decisions with respect to safety and pollution prevention and to request the Company's assistance as may be necessary.*

The Code describes specific responsibilities which should be defined for the master:

1. Implementing the safety and environmental protection policy of the Company.

2. Motivating the crew in the observation of that policy.

3. Issuing appropriate orders and instructions in a clear and simple manner.

4. Verifying that specified requirements are met.

5. Reviewing the SMS and reporting its deficiencies to the shore-based management.

This list of responsibilities has two important implications for the way a ship's safety management system is intended to work.

First, it must be **active**. It is a mechanism for putting the Company's policy into practice and making sure that it continues to operate effectively.

Second, it is about **improvement** – checking, reviewing and correcting deficiencies in how safety is managed on board.

Of course, although the Master has the overall responsibility for safety, he is not expected to do the whole job himself. He will delegate authority for particular activities to other officers and members of the crew.

The Safety Supervisor

Even though most Flag State Administrations require companies to have designated Safety Supervisors on their ships, they will not specify these individuals' responsibilities in great detail. Within the principles set out in international and national regulations and codes of practice, and taking into account the type, size and trading patterns of the ships in their fleet, each shipping company must decide what they want their Safety Supervisors to achieve.

Most important, the Master and Safety Supervisor on each ship must agree the nature of that person's work.

The best way to do this is to produce a simple, written description of the Safety Supervisor's job. Here is a guideline framework for doing so.

SAFETY SUPERVISOR Job Description	
Job purpose	*For example:* *The Safety Supervisor shall take care of the interests of the employees in matters concerning the work environment onboard. The Safety Supervisor shall see that the work onboard is performed in such a manner that due consideration is given to the safety and health of the employees. Where necessary, he will make proposals for new safety measures.* *Tasks within the responsibility of the Safety Supervisor may include:* • *Ensuring that machinery, equipment, chemical agents and work procedures do not expose employees to hazards.* • *Ensuring that personal protection devices and accident prevention equipment is in good condition and is used.* • *Ensuring that employees receive the required familiarisation, instruction, training and practice.* • *Ensuring that work is organised to enable employees to carry it out in a manner consistent with the requirements of health and safety.*
Job structure	
• Authority	*Limits of the Safety Supervisor's authority (for example, actions about which he must consult the Master in advance)*
• Other responsibilities	*Modifications to the Safety Supervisor's existing work to allow him time to carry out his safety duties*
• Working relationships	*Relationships with officers, particularly Heads of Departments*
• Reporting	*Arrangements for providing information about safety to the Master (for example, meeting frequency; regular reports)*

Job responsibilities	
• Safety training	*Organisation; delivery; records; shipboard familiarisation, shared responsibility with officers*
• Drills	*Planning; carrying out; assessing effectiveness, shared responsibility with officers*
• Safety Representatives	*Details of working relationships*
• Safety Committee	*Administration*
• Risk assessment	*Planning; carrying out; reporting; shared responsibility with officers*
• Safety inspections	*Planning; carrying out; reporting; shared responsibility with officers*
• Safety equipment	*Monitoring of provision and maintenance; shared responsibility with officers*
• Permit to work systems	*Monitoring of effective operation*
• Accident investigations	*Carrying out; reporting*
• Emergency procedures	*Monitoring of effective operation*
• Other	

You will find a blank version of this framework Job Description in **Section 2 – Tools for improving safety**. Use this to describe and agree the role of the Safety Supervisor on your ship.

1.1.3 Safety Representatives

As their title suggests, particular groups of the crew (such as catering personnel on passenger ships) are required, in certain administrations, to have their own Safety Representatives to represent their interests in matters of safety and health.

To be effective, their role should be:

- **Active**. They must be involved in monitoring and improving safety.

- **2-way**. Representatives should play a key role in ensuring that information and ideas about safe working practices pass in both directions between officers and ratings.

1.1.4 The Safety Committee

The membership of the Safety Committee may be specified by your administration or, failing that, by your company.

As an example, on Scandinavian registered ships the committee usually consists of the Master, the Safety Supervisor, up to three Safety Representatives (depending upon the size of the crew), the Chief Engineer, the Chief Steward and the Safety Officer if there is one.

The committee's purpose is to help make the ship a safe and healthy environment for all members of the crew. Its particular concerns are:

- **Risk assessment**

  Ensuring that work and living places and conditions which contain hazards to health or risk of accidents are systematically identified and actions taken to minimise or remove any dangers which are present.

- **Information**

  Receiving and disseminating information about safety and health issues, such as the results of risk assessments, safety inspections and accident investigations.

- **Training**

  Ensuring that new employees are given adequate familiarisation, instruction and training in safety matters, and that this relates to the particular risks faced by each individual concerned. Contributing actively to making safety an integral part of training at work.

- **Accident investigation**

  Examining and discussing all reports concerning accidents, injuries and 'near misses'. Seeking the causes of injury, sickness and death which may be linked to the environment on board, and discussing proposals for preventive measures. (To be effective, the Committee must have access to, and be able to review, any relevant reports, such as those resulting from the regular maintenance inspections specified in Chapter 10 of the ISM Code).

- **Ideas and improvements**

  In general, to discuss and agree ideas for improving safety on board and follow-up and monitor the consequences of actions taken.

The Safety Supervisor and all members of the Safety Committee must be familiar with current regulations, instructions and recommendations applying to safety and health on board.

1.2 STRUCTURE

1.2.1 Safety Representatives

There are three decisions to be taken if your Company is either required or, in the absence of a regulation to do so, has decided to have Safety Representatives on board.

1. Election vs Appointment

It is better for representatives to be elected by their fellow seafarers, rather than being appointed. Election gives their position status and authority. It also makes it clear who they represent. Note that some Flag States do not permit appointment of Safety Representatives, even by the Master.

2. Numbers

The number of safety representatives required will obviously depend on the size of the crew. You may find your Administration's regulations specify the minimum number you must have. For example, the requirements for United Kingdom and Norwegian registered ships are as follows (UK figures are from their MCA - Maritime and Coastguard Agency - Code of Safe Working Practices for Seafarers. The Norwegian figures are from the Norwegian Maritime Administration's Safety and Health Regulation of 4 August, 2000.)

United Kingdom		Norway	
6 – 15 crew	1 elected by officers and ratings	8 – 14 crew	1 elected by the ratings
16+ crew	1 elected by the officers+ 1 elected by the ratings	15 – 39 crew	2 elected by the ratings*
30+ ratings	1 elected by the officers + 3 elected by the ratings	more than 40 crew	3 elected by the ratings*
		*One of these representatives acts as Safety Supervisor	

3. Distribution

With the exception of ships with very small crews it is good practice to make sure that the different operational areas of the ship – deck, engine room, galley and so on - are all represented.

1.2.2 The Safety Committee

Here are the main issues which you must resolve to make your Safety Committee work effectively.

1. Membership

In addition to the permanent members of the Committee, it is often helpful to invite others to attend particular meetings. For example, if you have contractors' personnel on board it is a statutory requirement in some Administrations for them to provide a representative. Even if you are not obliged to do this, it is good practice.

If you have carried out a safety inspection or risk assessment in a particular area of the ship, ask the Head of Department to come to the meeting and take part in the discussion of the report.

2. Roles

Normally the meeting will be chaired by the Master. The Safety Supervisor will play a leading role in providing information.

Encourage the Safety Representatives to play as active a part in the meetings as possible. For example, when a Safety Representative has been involved in a safety inspection in his area of the ship invite him to present at least part of the report.

3. Large ships and ferries

To enable discussions to be effective, Safety Committees must be kept to a reasonable size, say not more than ten people. Ships, such as cruise liners, with large crews should set up committees for each area. The main ship's Safety Committee will consist of a representative from each of these.

On ferries with crews who work shifts the committee structure must enable each shift to contribute to improving safety and allow lessons learned on one shift to be communicated to the others.

4. Safety Committee meetings

- **Frequency**

    This will depend on the circumstances and trading pattern of each ship and also any minimum frequency specified by your Administration. For example, on Norwegian registered ships there must be no fewer than six meetings per year (with a recommended frequency of one a month). In addition, the Safety Committee should hold as many open meetings as possible for all those working onboard.

    Common sense will often be the best judge of when to hold meetings, for example soon after sailing and before docking or prior to formal audits and inspections.

- **Agendas**

    - **Source of items**. Many of the items on the agenda will come from the Safety Supervisor and the Company. However it is important to encourage members of the crew to submit issues for discussion through their Safety Representatives.

    - **Submitting items**. Agree a cut-off time for submission of items for discussion. For example, if items are submitted not less than 2 weeks before the meeting, the agenda can be produced and circulated 1 week beforehand, giving everyone attending sufficient time to think about the issues. Use 'Any other business' to deal with issues which come up at short notice.

    - **Structure and detail**. Important items should go early the agenda, rather than at the end, so that sufficient time is devoted to them. Include enough detail to enable committee members to prepare. For

11

example, let people know if a decision has to be made about a particular issue so that they can think about it and, if necessary, consult those they represent.

> **A balance of review and planning**. It is important both to review what has happened since the previous meeting and to discuss what is planned before the next one.

> **Publicity**. In addition to circulating agendas to those who will be taking part in the meeting, give copies to Heads of Department and display them where the remainder of the crew will see them. The Company may also require a copy.

• **Minutes**

These should be brief summaries, but they must include any actions agreed, the person responsible for carrying them out and timescales for completion. Produce and circulate the minutes as soon as possible after the meeting. As with agendas, display them where they can be read by crew members. Your shore office will normally require a copy.

Here are typical examples of an agenda and minutes.

M/S – – – – – – –
Health and Safety Committee

Circulation

Master
Safety Supervisor/Safety Officer
Chief Engineer
Chief Steward
Other Safety Representatives

Meeting of the Safety Committee, date …….., time ……, location…………
Agenda

1. **Minutes of previous meeting** (copy attached)

2. **Matters arising**

3. **Tasks for periodic/voyage planning:**
   • Mooring operations

4. **Accidents or near misses reported since last meeting**
   • Injury by fall on slippery floor in galley in heavy weather: date …
   • Complaints of dizziness experienced when using new 'superpaint' in provision room
   Discussion/decision about prevention of future problems

5. **Demonstration of training video on fire-fighting drills**
   Discussion of whether/how to use this on board

6. **Any other business**

7. **Date of the next meeting**

<table>
<tr><td colspan="2" align="center">**M/S — — — — — —**
Health and Safety Committee

Meeting of the Safety Committee, date …, time …, location…………
Minutes</td></tr>
<tr><td colspan="2">**Present**
Master (Chair)
Safety Supervisor / Safety Officer
Chief Engineer
Chief Steward
Other Safety Representatives</td></tr>
</table>

	Action
1. Minutes of previous meeting	
Accepted as an accurate record and signed by the Master.	File. Safety Supervisor. Immediate.
2. Matters arising	
There were no matters arising	
3. Tasks for periodic/voyage planning	
Working operations for mooring: Inspection of anchoring / mooring windlass revealed that the locking pin for the gear handle was missing (chain broken), creating a possible risk of freeing the transmission connection. A temporary locking pin has been made in the workshop - with chain.	
A replacement has been ordered from the supplier. Delivery 6 weeks. Receipt of replacement to be confirmed at the next meeting	Chief Engineer to report.
4. Accidents or near misses reported since last meeting	
Injury by fall on slippery floor in galley in heavy rolling: Safety Supervisor reported that the accident investigation revealed that the skid protection layer in front of the galley was worn out. A new skid protection layer has been fitted.	
Complaints of dizziness experienced when using new 'superpaint' in provision room: The Safety Supervisor reported that the boxes containing this paint are missing the required paint category or content declaration. This violates both company and statutory instruction for the provision of paint and other hazardous substances. The paint should have been refused on delivery.	Safety Supervisor to liase with HoD to have paint clearly marked 'Only to be used in open areas'. Immediate.
It was decided that:	
• the rest of the paint in store will only be used in open areas (not in closed compartments)	Master to e-mail Purchasing Dept ashore. Immediate.
• shore office to be informed about the breaking of the purchase instructions for ships' paints.	
5. Demonstration of training video on fire-fighting drills	
The video was very good and relevant for our shipboard conditions. It was agreed to keep it on board and arrange short training sessions using it for all crew involved.	Safety Supervisor to organise timetable for sessions and agree with HoDs. Programme to be agreed in 2 weeks.
6. Any other business	
There was no other business.	
The meeting was adjourned at … pm. The next meeting will be on …	

1.2.3 Plans and instructions

The ISM Code says that:

The Company should establish procedures for the preparation of plans and instructions for key shipboard operations concerning the safety of the ship and the prevention of pollution. The various tasks involved should be defined and assigned to qualified personnel.

The Code does not attempt to define or list what is covered by 'key shipboard operations'. That task is left, not only to companies, but more significantly to national Administrations, many of whom lay down very detailed regulations and recommendations. The UK MCA's Code, for example, is several hundred pages long and contains 28 chapters covering activities as diverse as food preparation and anchoring.

The set of documents on each ship which contain the various plans and instructions relevant to that vessel are often referred to as the ship's Safety Management Manual. To prevent safety management on board turning into a paperwork nightmare, companies, together with ships' Masters and officers, must ensure that:

- The appropriate documents are easy to access for those who need to refer to them.

- They are written in language that is as clear and simple as possible.

- There is a system for reviewing and updating them, including, when necessary, discarding those that are obsolete.

1.2.4 Public display of safety information

For certain safety information, ease of access means more than simply filing it in a convenient place. It must be publicly displayed, both to reassure those on board that the ship conforms to particular regulations and to remind them of specific safety duties and precautions.

The content and display of two of the most important types of safety information – Muster Lists and emergency instructions – are a statutory requirement under the SOLAS Convention.

Most national Administrations have their own, additional regulations. For example, Norwegian registered ships must display:

1. Fire control plan

2. Muster lists, posted in conspicuous places

3. Operating instructions for life-saving appliances, posted on the embarkation deck

4. Safe manning document, posted in a conspicuous place

5. Display of ships manoeuvring information (for ships over 10,000 grt.)

6. Distress Procedure/GMDSS. Notice at radio-operational panel or bridge

7. Warning notice for helicopter operations (ships with helicopter deck/platform)

8. Warning of excessive noise level at entrance to relevant spaces (need for ear protection)

9. Warning notice for gas under pressure at entrance of compartment

10. Warning notice for radar post

11. Warning notice for lack of oxygen/poisonous gas etc.

12. Gas-fired installations, instructions for use

13. Safety lamps regulation, copy in crew cabins

14. Exemption certificate (dispensation for ship's overtime regulations)

For cargo ships

15. The safety construction certificate (prominent/accessible place)

16. The safety equipment certificate (prominent/accessible place)

17. The safety radio certificate (prominent/accessible place)

18. Damage control plan on navigating bridge (ships over 500 grt.)

For ships carrying dangerous cargo

19. Possible health hazard posters in all mess rooms (Norwegian/English)

20. Cargo warning notice posted at the gangway

1.3 PROCEDURES

The ISM Code states that each company's safety management system must include:

Instructions and procedures to ensure safe operation of ships and protection of the environment in compliance with relevant international and Flag State legislation

The result of this regulation is that ships should now have a Safety Management Manual covering most operations on board. Following this will, of itself, make work on board safer.

In addition there are five procedures whose specific aim is the general improvement of safe working practices and it is these which this section of the manual will now cover. They are:

• Risk assessment

• Safety inspections

• Permit to work systems

- Drills

- Accident and near miss investigations

1.3.1   Risk assessment (IMO refer to this as 'Formal Safety Assessment' – FSA)

People who work in potentially dangerous occupations, such as shipping, are usually conscious of the dangers they face and as they become more experienced they get better at assessing the risks of particular situations at work. But the approach to risk assessment which safety management systems include is very different from one that simply relies on individuals becoming more aware of the hazards as they get better at their jobs.

1. **What is Risk Assessment?**

   Risk assessment is a formal procedure for identifying hazards, assessing the seriousness of the risk they pose, selecting actions to eliminate these risks or reduce them to an acceptable level, implementing these actions and monitoring their effectiveness.

   It is a procedure which can be applied to every type of potentially dangerous situation including, for example, navigational hazards at sea and a shipping company's exposure to currency fluctuations. In this manual we will confine ourselves to hazards which can damage the health and safety of members of the crew.

2. **When should Risk Assessment be carried out?**

   The EU Standard covering the working environment, health and safety of workers on board ship answers that question as follows:

   > 1. Risk Assessment shall be made on a regular basis and:
   >
   >   a) whenever new working equipment or new technology is introduced
   >
   >   b) whenever other modifications are made to the organization or planning of the work, which may affect the health and safety of workers.
   >
   > 2. The result of the risk assessment shall be documented in writing.
   >
   >   If a risk to the safety and heath of workers is identified, the necessary measures shall be taken to eliminate or reduce such risk.

3. **Who should carry out Risk Assessments?**

   The Company has the overall responsibility for setting up standard procedures for carrying out Risk Assessments and making sure that they are recorded, implemented and followed up.

   Under the ISM Code each Company has a legal obligation to do so. (Chapter 1.2.2. '*Safety management objectives of the Company should......establish safeguards against all identified risks*').

On each ship it is the Master's responsibility to ensure that these procedures are put into practice. Safety Supervisors and Safety Representatives will play an important part in doing the actual assessments, but it is very important to involve those seafarers who work on the activities being assessed. No-one knows the dangers of a particular job better than those who do it every day.

4. How does Risk Assessment work?

The details of Risk Assessment systems will vary from company to company, but the principles on which they are based are the same. They are:

- **Prioritisation.** Decide which activities, in which areas of the ship, to assess.

- **Identification.** Systematically identify the hazards of the activity chosen for assessment.

- **Evaluation.** Decide upon the level of risk which each hazard presents.

- **Action.** Decide what, if anything, to do about the risk and implement that decision.

- **Verification.** Monitor the actions taken.

Let's look at these in more detail.

- **Prioritisation**

  Remember that the focus of Risk Assessment is on activities, not just areas of the ship. So, for example, you will assess the hazards of loading and discharging cargo and not simply the cargo holds.

  Your aim must be to assess all of the significant hazards on board, but clearly you will use your professional judgement to prioritise these. As you do so, think about:

  ➢ **Change.** New equipment and modified procedures can create new dangers.

  ➢ **Infrequent activities.** Don't confine assessment to familiar, day to day operations.

- **Identification**

  What is the difference between a hazard and a risk? To quote the UK MCA's definitions:

  ➢ A hazard is a source of potential harm or damage or a situation with potential for harm or damage.

  ➢ Risk has two elements – the likelihood that a hazard may occur and the consequences of the hazardous event.

  For example, using a chicken grill in the galley is a hazard.

- **Evaluation**

  This particular hazard presents the risk of fire. Is there likely to be a fire? Probably not, but the consequences if there were could be serious.

  Risk Assessment is very much about asking *what if* questions and then making a judgement about the severity of the risk by balancing the likelihood and the consequences.

  One major advantage of doing this systematically is that it alerts us to hazards which, though extremely unlikely, might have disastrous consequences. Why, for example, do ships prepare their anchors for lowering when manoeuvring to come alongside in a busy harbour? Because although main engine failure is most unlikely the consequences if it did happen could be very severe.

- **Action**

  Once the hazards have been identified and the risks assessed we can objectively decide what to do about them. Possible actions fall into one of four categories – the 4Ts.

  ➢ **Terminate.** There are some hazards which pose so severe a risk that the only sensible step is to remove them entirely by, for example, changing procedures or materials. Poisonous chemicals may be replaced by non-poisonous alternatives. Early airships were filled with hydrogen, which is highly explosive, while modern ones use helium, which is not explosive at all.

  ➢ **Treat.** This is the most common approach to risks which are reasonably likely and have consequences which are unpleasant, though not catastrophic. Normal precautions are simply not enough. Something has to be added or changed in order to make the risk acceptable. So we install safeguards to reduce the likelihood of the hazard occurring and provide equipment, such as fire extinguishers, to reduce the consequences if it does.

  ➢ **Tolerate.** Some risks are both unlikely and have trivial consequences. We can tolerate these, so long as we take the normal precautions, such as using the correct personal protection equipment or choosing an appropriate person to do the job.

  ➢ **Transfer.** It may be possible, in some cases, to transfer the risk to someone else who, perhaps, has special competence in the area concerned. For example, specialist travelling squads can be brought on board to carry out difficult hot work. Of course, though this transfers the physical risk, the legal responsibility remains with the ship's Master and the company. Proper insurance would be necessary to guard against the financial risks of an accident.

  Once the severity of the risk has been assessed there will normally be a range of possible actions available to reduce either the likelihood or the consequences or both. Factors to consider when choosing the best option in the circumstances are:

> ➤ **The ability to control the hazard.** For example, it may be possible to use less hazardous materials or provide special protective equipment or install guards or give those involved special training.

> ➤ **The cost of reducing the hazard.** Cost should never be a reason for tolerating a hazard which poses even a moderately severe risk, but it may result in a decision to treat a hazard, rather than attempting to terminate it.

> ➤ **The amount of effort required to reduce the risk.** Be careful! If the proposed action is too complicated, particularly if it involves individuals taking very elaborate, time consuming precautions, they may be tempted to cut corners and ignore the risks.

• **Verification**

It is extremely important to follow up the actions taken to make sure, first that they are being implemented as intended and second that they do, in fact, reduce the risk.

A risk assessment of the chicken grilling example can be summarised as follows.

Risk factors	Low	Some	Medium	High
Likelihood Fire is certainly possible, particularly in adverse weather conditions.			X	
Consequences Any fire on board ship can have serious consequences.				X
Ability to control the hazard Though the hazard cannot be completely eliminated without taking chicken off the menu, there are a number of possible controls available, such as a clear operating procedure, appropriate training for those who use the griller and the provision of a portable fire extinguisher.			X	
Cost of reducing the hazard None of the appropriate actions are particularly expensive.		X		
Effort required to reduce the risk Very little effort is involved.	X			

Safety Inspections

Regular safety inspections are another important method for maintaining and improving safety on board. There are certain features which they share with Risk Assessment, but there are also distinctions between the two procedures.

They share the same aim – to improve safety. They both use systematic observation; they are both recorded; and they both provide the basis for action and improvement.

The principal differences between the two are:

- Safety inspections focus on areas of the ship, whereas Risk Assessment looks at activities.

- Safety inspections examine existing circumstances and practices, whereas Risk Assessment asks *what if* questions.

- Safety inspections should be used to highlight and acknowledge good practice, as well as identifying problems, an aim which does not form part of a Risk Assessment.

The details of an effective programme of safety inspections will depend on the type and circumstances of each ship but, in every case, it will involve:

- Planning the programme.

- Carrying out the inspections.

- Reporting the findings.

- Following up any actions taken.

1. **Planning the programme**

    - **Where to inspect**

        All areas of the ship normally accessible to the crew must be inspected. The first step in designing a programme of inspections is to list the different working and living areas on board and put them in priority order for inspection.

    - **Frequency**

        The design of the inspection programme must ensure that all areas are inspected within a reasonable timescale. Some Flag States stipulate how often each area must be inspected. For example, on UK registered ships the interval between inspection of each area must not be more than three months. Many shipping companies have similar regulations.

- **What to inspect**

  Every inspection should cover:

  ➢ **Working/living environment** – for example, ease of entry and exit, marking of hazards, state of guards and handrails, lighting, ventilation and noise levels, safe stowage of tools and materials, general cleanliness and tidiness.

  ➢ **Working/living practices** – for example, working within established procedures and regulations, use of personal protective equipment, levels of supervision, levels of training.

  ➢ **Examples of good practice.** Safety inspections can easily be seen as heavy handed 'policing' activities. Plan your inspections to 'catch people doing something right'.

  ➢ **Progress and action.** Improvement comes from building on the results of previous inspections. Use the last inspection report to help plan the next one.

- **Who to involve**

  Heads of Department and Safety Representatives should be consulted when planning safety inspections and involved in carrying them out

2. **Carrying out safety inspections**

   An effective safety inspection should be:

- **Systematic**

  The best way to achieve this is to use checklists. You will find a range of these in **Section 2 – Tools for improving safety**. Modify and add to these to suit the circumstances of your ship.

- **Consistent**

  Checklists also help in achieving consistency, as does reviewing the results of previous inspections at the planning stage.

- **Positive**

  During the inspection congratulate people about examples of good practice and avoid blaming them for unsafe acts and conditions. Instead remind them of the consequences of these and the benefits – to them – of working safely.

3. Reporting the findings

Safety inspection reports should be:

- **Concise and standardised**

  Busy people tend not to read reports which are too long. A standard format makes it easy to compare one report with another and identify progress and improvement.

- **Action**

  The report must say who is going to take what action and by when.

- **Communicated**

  Written copies of the report should go to:

  ➤ The Master and, through him, the Company

  ➤ The relevant Head of Department and Safety Representative

  ➤ The Safety Committee.

  The report will also be an item for discussion at the next Safety Committee meeting. In addition, there should be a method for reporting the findings, perhaps in summary form, to crew members in the area inspected.

4. Following up any actions taken

It is essential to make sure that the actions agreed are put into effect and also that they achieve the results intended.

1.3.3   Permit to Work systems

1. The purpose of Permit to Work systems

Some types of work cannot be carried out safely without a formal set of controls, understood by everyone involved and put into operation consistently and systematically every time the work is undertaken. The purpose of Permit to Work systems is to provide these controls.

2. The type of work covered by Permit to Work systems

These systems are particularly important for work which can only be done by suspending normal safety precautions, for example by removing guards from dangerous machinery.

On board ship, examples of the type of work covered will include:

- Entering enclosed spaces

- Hot work/Cold work

- Working overside and aloft

- Electrical maintenance (for non-professionals)

- Pipeline breaking

- Working on pressure vessels and in cargo tanks

This list is not intended to cover everything on every ship. Only a proper risk assessment can define every type of work which must be covered by a Permit to Work system.

3. **Those who operate Permit to Work systems**

If it is to be effective, the system must clearly define who is to be involved in operating it. There are two categories of people – those who authorise Permits and those who do the work.

To authorise a Permit to Work an individual must:

- Have appropriate seniority. On most ships, Permits can only be authorised by the Master, or by written delegation from him to a responsible Officer. (In certain administrations, it is a requirement that the Safety Supervisor counter-signs all Permits to Work.)

- Understand the nature of the work.

- Have the experience and ability to assess the risks involved.

Those who will carry out the work must:

- Be fully capable of doing the job involved. This may seem obvious, but it is the foundation on which the safe and successful completion of the work is based. No system, however perfect, can ensure the safety of someone who is not entirely sure about what he is doing.

- Understand, in detail, how the Permit to Work system operates. This can be a potential trap when work is to be carried out by contractor's staff or new crew members. They may have experience of other Permit to Work systems, but do they know precisely how yours operates?

- Work with the person authorising the Permit. Accepting a Permit to Work is not like buying a ticket in a theatre! It is essential for the person doing the work to contribute to the assessment of risks and the identification of precautions described on the Permit. Remember, it will be his life which will be at risk.

4. How Permit to Work systems operate

While the details of individual systems will depend on a variety of circumstances, particularly the type of ship involved, every system should contain the following steps.

- **Assess the risks**

  Follow the process for systematic risk assessment described earlier in this section of the manual. In particular:

  ➢ Ask '*what if ...*' questions. For example, what if the work has to be suspended for some reason, what if there is an emergency, what if the job takes much longer than anticipated?

  ➢ Think about the context of the work being planned. For example, if the task involves hot work in a particular cargo space, could this create a hazard for whatever is in the next one? Are there any other jobs being carried out under different Permits to Work which could be affected by this one?

  ➢ Don't be complacent. Just because this particular job has been done many times before, don't assume that the information on the previous Permit is still valid. Perhaps the equipment used will be different this time. Perhaps the physical setting will have changed. Perhaps the person doing the job is planning to tackle it in a slightly different way. Perhaps on this occasion the work will involve a shift changeover. Perhaps ... perhaps ... perhaps. Always look at each job with a fresh eye.

- **Issue the Permit**

  Once again, this is a two way process. Both the person authorising the Permit and the person accepting it must be 100% satisfied that the information it contains will enable the work to be carried out safely. (Be aware of any time limitation on the Permit - see 'The content of the Permit' below)

  The contents of the Permit are dealt with below.

- **Prepare the work**

  There will be situations when this will be the most time consuming part of the job. It is essential not to rush preparation or cut corners. Typical preparatory work includes:

  ➢ Disconnecting electrical power supplies.

  ➢ Prominently displaying the Permit and warning signs.

  ➢ Testing and putting on appropriate personal protective equipment.

  ➢ Ensuring that rescue equipment and personnel are in place.

➢ Fencing off work areas.

➢ Ensuring that everyone involved in or affected by the work has been thoroughly briefed and that there are proper arrangements for supervision.

This is not, of course, intended to be a comprehensive list.

- **Carry out the work**

  If those doing the job are competent and the previous three steps have been done correctly, the work should go safely and smoothly. But watch out for the unexpected – a piece of equipment that fails, the need to fetch an additional tool. If anything arises which has not been anticipated when completing the Permit, stop and think. Sometimes it may be necessary to review the Permit with the person who authorised it before proceeding.

- **Formally complete the process**

  Once the work has been satisfactorily completed, the final step is to return everything to normal and sign off the Permit. This involves:

  ➢ Replacing any permanent precautions, such as guards on machines, which were removed to do the work.

  ➢ Removing the warnings and temporary precautions, such as those used to fence off the work area.

  ➢ Ensuring that rescue and personal protection equipment is checked after use and put back in the proper place.

  ➢ Formally handing the workplace back to those who normally work there.

  ➢ Signing off the Permit and ensuring that it is properly filed. Don't forget to review how the work went and, in particular, whether any lessons could be learned for the next time that similar work has to be carried out.

5. **The content of the Permit**

   The permit-to-work form must help communication between everyone involved. It should be designed by the company issuing the permit, taking into account individual site conditions and requirements. Separate permit forms may be required for different tasks, such as hot work and entry into confined spaces, so that sufficient emphasis can be given to the particular hazards present and precautions required.

   The essential elements of a permit-to-work form are listed in the diagram below. This is reproduced with kind permission from the UK's Health and Safety Executive. If your permit does not cover these elements it is unlikely to be fully achieving its purpose.

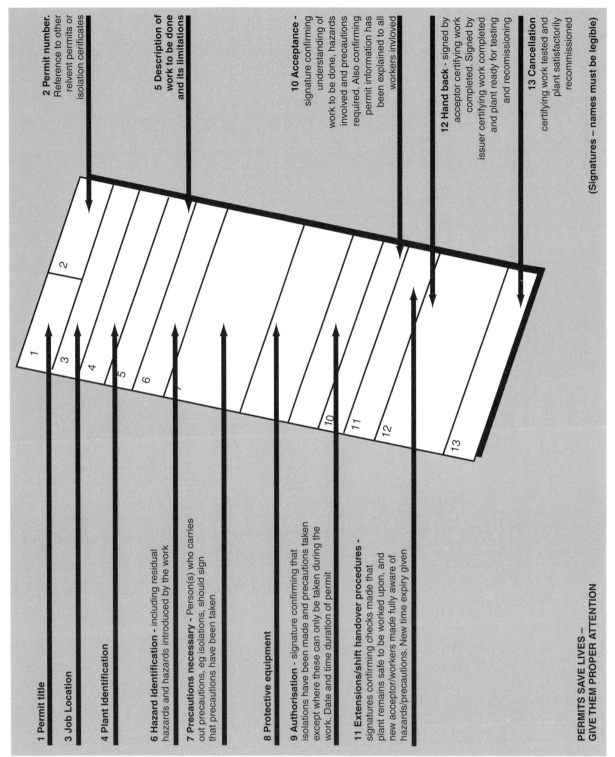

1 Permit title

2 Permit number. Reference to other relevent permits or isolation cerificates

3 Job Location

4 Plant Identification

5 Description of work to be done and its limitations

6 Hazard Identification - including residual hazards and hazards introduced by the work

7 Precautions necessary - Person(s) who carries out precautions, eg isolations, should sign that precautions have been taken

8 Protective equipment

9 Authorisation - signature confirming that isolations have been made and precautions taken except where these can only be taken during the work. Date and time duration of permit

10 Acceptance - signature confirming understanding of work to be done, hazards involved and precautions required. Also confirming permit information has been explained to all workers involved

11 Extensions/shift handover procedures - signatures confirming checks made that plant remains safe to be worked upon, and new acceptor/workers made fully aware of hazards/precautions. New time expiry given

12 Hand back - signed by acceptor certifying work completed. Signed by issuer certifying work completed and plant ready for testing and recomissioning

13 Cancellation certifying work tested and plant satisfactorily recommissioned

(Signatures – names must be legible)

**PERMITS SAVE LIVES –
GIVE THEM PROPER ATTENTION**

(By kind permission of the United Kingdom Health & Safety Executive)

Note that limiting the duration of the permit is often a particularly important safety precaution. Some administrations' guidelines will specify, for example, 'not more than 12 hours for work in confined spaces/tanks'. Check your own national regulations for requirements of this type.

1.3.4 Drills

Everyone hopes that a combination of systematic risk assessment, regular safety inspections and safe working practices, including Permit to Work systems, will keep the ship and its crew safe. But emergencies can still happen and the crew must be prepared to deal with them effectively if they do. That is why drills are an essential part of a ship's safety system.

1. Types of drills

Under Chapter III of the SOLAS Convention ships are legally required to carry out regular fire and abandon ship drills. The Convention details what these must cover and how often they must be carried out. Since every ship must have a copy of SOLAS on board, these details are not reproduced here. In addition, some national Administrations have even more detailed regulations and recommendations covering fire and abandon ship drills.

Note: There is a common misinterpretation of the SOLAS regulations related to abandon ship drills (Chapter III, Regulation 19, 3.3.3). It is not the case that lifeboat launching shall be carried out with all the assigned ratings on board. As this is a test, only 'assigned operating crew' holding Lifeboat Proficiency Certificates are allowed to operate the lifeboats.

Other types of drill will include:

- Man overboard

- Rescue from an enclosed space

- Rescue of an injured crew member

- Emergency steering

- Excessive list

- Emergencies arising from the carriage of dangerous goods.

Again, this is not intended to be a comprehensive list.

There should be a logical, planned programme for carrying out all of the necessary drills, statutory and non-statutory. This programme should take into account training for emergencies, because training and drills are not the same thing.

2. Training and drills

It is important to recognise that there is a difference between training and drills. All crew members must learn how to tackle emergencies. That is what training is about. Once they have been trained, they must demonstrate that they can tackle the emergency properly. That is what drills are for.

Other differences between training and drills include:

The person in charge of a training session ...	The person in charge of a drill ...
• Will be a ship's officer, who ... • Acts as a *trainer*, explaining how to deal with the emergency and providing help, information and advice to those taking part **A training session may be run ...** • In a series of stages, with a pause for discussion and instruction between each stage. Sometimes the trainer will ask those taking part to carry out an activity slowly before working up to the required speed **When training goes badly ...** • We identify what went wrong and apply the lessons to help us improve	• Will be the responsible ship's officer acting as an observer, defining the ground rules for the drill and then watching to see how well it is being carried out • A Port State Control Officer who may only act as an observer **A drill will always be run ...** • At normal pace and without interruption (unless to continue would be dangerous for those taking part or other crew members) **When training goes badly ...** • The ship may be detained if the drill has been part of a Port State Inspection

3. **How to run an effective drill**

There are four stages – preparation, briefing, observation and de-briefing.

Preparation

- **Information you require**

  ➢ **Review the notes** from the previous drill.

- **Decisions you must take**

  ➢ **What type** of drill to run.

  ➢ **When to do it.** Emergencies sometimes happen at night. Some drills should test the crew's ability to carry out emergency procedures during the hours of darkness.

  ➢ **Who to involve.** It is important (and mandatory in the case of fire and abandon ship drills) for all crew members to take part.

  ➢ **Where to hold it.** Fire drills, for example, will often be held in obvious places such as the galley, but don't ignore the less obvious ones. Fire teams must be able to tackle fires wherever they start.

  ➢ **How to make the drill realistic.** Ways of doing this include removing the team leader in the middle of the drill to see how the rest of the team cope; not allowing those taking part to use normal entrances, staircases and so on; ensuring that, over a period of time, the programme of drills involves the use of all the ship's safety equipment.

- **Safety precautions you must take**

  - ➤ **Do a risk assessment of each drill.** Make sure that equipment is properly maintained and operates correctly. Don't add too much realism to drills of any type. Be particularly careful of methods, such as the use of smoke machines or masks, which restrict visibility.

  - ➤ **Take weather conditions into account.** The intention of drills is to ensure the safety of the ship and its crew. They should not present any inherent hazard to those taking part. Certain drills should not be held during adverse weather conditions.

  - ➤ **Decide whether to give prior notice of the drill.** The less warning people get, the more realistic the drill will be. But providing no warning at all may be unacceptably dangerous under certain conditions.

  - ➤ **Distinguish between lifeboat mustering and lifeboat launching.** It is quite common to combine abandon ship drills – mustering - with SOLAS drills in which the lifeboats are lowered and, on occasions, launched with the 'survival craft crew' onboard.

    It is a terrible and totally unacceptable fact that this combined procedure has resulted in a large number of deaths and injuries over the past few years. Launching is intended to be a drill/verification of the proficiency of the qualified 'assigned operating crew' of the lifeboat and should not be extended to include the entire 'survival crew' (or passengers).

  - ➤ **Distinguish between drills and the testing of technical appliances.** Shipboard drills such as abandon ship and fire fighting must not be confused with the functional testing of technical appliances or equipment (even if the drills may sometimes reveal malfunctions). The maintenance, inspection and testing of safety appliances is a separate part of the maintenance programme and is intended to ensure that the equipment is in proper working condition *before* the drills take place.

Briefing

Before taking part in the drill, those involved should be briefed about:

- **What the drill is for** and the standard they are expected to achieve. Drills are just like any other task. They will not go well if those involved are unclear about their objectives.

- **How the drill will be run.** Of course, variations may be introduced during the drill to add realism.

- **How the previous drill of this type went.** It is important to emphasise what went well and not just what aspects need to be improved.

- **How to ensure that the drill is safe.** Those taking part must understand the hazards, the precautions and – very important – the order they will be given if it is necessary to stop the drill.

Observation

- **Throughout the drill** watch for:

  - ➤ **Timescales.** The drill has to be done correctly, but doing it too slowly can lead to disaster in real emergencies.

  - ➤ **What goes well.** It is all too easy to concentrate on mistakes, but it is at least as important for those taking part to understand what they have done well.

  - ➤ **Improvements.** While drills are not training sessions, they almost always provide lessons which will lead to better performance the next time around, whether that is another drill or a real emergency.

- **At the beginning of the drill,** watch for:

  - ➤ **How the leader behaves.** Does he give clear instructions? Does he assign work to individuals correctly? Does he ensure that everyone is involved? Does he check that everyone understands?

  - ➤ **How the team behaves.** Do they pay attention? Do they ask appropriate questions?

- **During the drill,** watch for:

  - ➤ **Communication.** Are instructions delivered clearly? Do team members listen to one another?

  - ➤ **Atmosphere.** Do those taking part behave calmly or is there evidence of confusion or panic?

  - ➤ **Teamwork.** Do team members help one another? Do they watch out for one another?

  - ➤ **Adaptability.** How do they cope with any unexpected problems, such as having the leader removed from the team or finding that they cannot use the normal entrance to a particular area?

  - ➤ **Correct use of equipment.** Is the right equipment used and is it used correctly?

- **At the end of the drill,** watch for:

  - ➤ **How the leader behaves (again).** Does he use praise and encouragement to strengthen the team?

  - ➤ **Success!** Did the drill achieve its objective?

De-briefing

- **Once the drill is over:**

  - ➢ **Review your notes.** Decide on the successes and improvements which you will want to highlight in the de-briefing session.

  - ➢ **Ask the group how they thought the drill went.** Encourage them to identify what went well, before focussing on any mistakes.

  - ➢ **Add your own comments.** Try to make this as much of a discussion as you can. People learn much more from being encouraged to think through what they have done themselves than they do from simply being told by someone else.

  - ➢ **Avoid personalising criticism.** Be as descriptive as possible, particularly when you are talking about things which didn't go too well. People can change their behaviour much more easily than they can change their personalities!

  - ➢ **Give them hope!** It is essential, particularly when drills go badly, for the team to see how they can do better next time.

  - ➢ **Remind them that 'next time' may be a real emergency.**

1.3.5   Accident and 'near miss' investigations

1. **The legal requirements**

   Chapter 9 of the ISM Code says:

   9.1 The SMS should include procedures ensuring that non-conformities, accidents and hazardous situations are reported to the Company, investigated and analysed with the objective of improving safety and pollution prevention.

   9.2 The Company should establish procedures for the implementation of corrective action.

   As with so many other parts of the Code, national administrations have created much more detailed regulations and recommendations around these two general requirements.

2. **Definitions and the focus of this manual**

   - A 'non-conformity' is any situation on board which does not meet the requirements of the Code, such as the absence of an established procedure for reporting accidents.

   - In the regulations of most national administrations the term 'accident' covers damage to the ship and its cargo and pollution of the environment, as well as injury to individuals. Since this manual focuses on occupational health and safety, we use the word 'accident' to mean personal injury only.

31

- A 'hazardous occurrence' is an event or situation which might have resulted in an accident but, very often by sheer luck, did not. For example, a spanner dropped by someone working aloft is a hazardous occurrence when it lands harmlessly on the deck. When it kills a passing crew member, that is an accident!

We prefer the term 'near miss' and that is what will be used from now on.

3. Why investigate near misses?

There are two reasons. First, it is the law. The second, better, reason for doing so is that experience, backed by research, tells us that serious and fatal accidents are the tip of an iceberg whose base is an enormous number of near misses.

This phenomenon is often called the 'Heinrich Distribution Triangle' after D W Heinrich who carried out the first research on it in the 1930s. Though the exact proportions of each slice of the triangle do vary depending on the activity studied, the principle is always the same.

Here are some typical figures from an American study carried out in the shipping industry.

Event	Heinrich's distribution	Average frequency onboard
Serious personal injury	1	Seldom
Minor personal injury/ Property damage	30	Frequent
Near misses	300	Twice daily

4. Near miss investigation – a huge opportunity

Unfortunately, it is very common for ISM Code audits on board to reveal that there has been no reporting of near misses whatsoever, despite the fact that a glance at the medical records reveal a number of minor injuries which have been medically treated.

Given that there is a clearly established relationship between the enormous volume of near misses and the very limited number of serious accidents, investigating near misses and acting on what those investigations reveal offers a huge opportunity to make ships safer.

5. The purposes of accident and near miss investigations

There are three different reasons for investigating accidents and near misses:

- **The law**

  This procedure is mandatory under both the ISM Code and the laws and regulations of national administrations.

32

- **Prevention**

  The most important purpose of these investigations is to find out what happened, identify the causes and take whatever steps are necessary to prevent similar events occurring in the future.

- **Facts – not Blame**

  On rare occasions accidents are caused by deliberate negligence and, when that is the case, the behaviour of those concerned cannot be overlooked. However, the danger of treating accident investigations as a 'policing' activity – a search for someone to blame – is that everyone involved can become very defensive and reluctant to co-operate. The result is that often the true causes never come to light and the prime purpose – prevention – is not achieved.

6. **How to carry out an accident or near miss investigation**

   - **The process**

     For simplicity's sake the process described below is for investigating accidents. Exactly the same principles apply to investigating near misses with the obvious exception of the references to the treatment of injuries.

   - **Preparation**

     Because accidents cannot be predicted it is essential for the person responsible for accident investigation to be ready to respond quickly. One practical step is to prepare a 'grab bag' containing, for example, a measuring tape, a torch, a light meter, a camera, a notebook and pens, a roll of 'tiger' tape, a hand held tape recorder and, if possible, a video camera.

     Experience tells us that people tend to 'borrow' items from the grab bag, so check its contents regularly!

   - **The basic procedure**

     Each shipping company will have its own procedure for carrying out these investigations. Though the details will differ, there are five basic steps:

     ➢ Respond to the accident

     ➢ Collect evidence

     ➢ Analyse the causes (immediate causes – basic causes – root causes)

     ➢ Plan, record and implement corrective action

     ➢ Monitor the action taken

In some situations there will be obvious corrective action which must be taken without delay. For example, if someone has been hurt by unguarded machinery, replace the guard as soon as possible.

- **Respond to the accident**

  ➤ When people have been hurt the priority is to ensure their safety, first at the site of the accident and, as quickly as possible, by removing them to a safe place for treatment.

  ➤ If it can be avoided, the person who will carry out the accident investigation should not get involved in helping the injured. It is very important to remain objective and start the investigation as soon as possible after the accident.

- **Collect evidence**

  Avoid jumping to conclusions at this stage. Stick to collecting evidence.

  ➤ There are three different types of evidence – observations of where the accident occurred; interview statements from witnesses, those injured and any others with useful information; and relevant documents.

  ➤ Make as detailed a record of the accident site as possible, including measurements, sketches, photographs and video footage. Remove or isolate any items, such as personal protective clothing, tools or materials, which may be used as evidence in the investigation.

  ➤ Record the names and, if necessary, addresses of witnesses. Identify anyone else with relevant information, such as those present when a particular order was given. Carry out the interviews as soon after the accident as possible, while those involved can still remember what happened.

  ➤ Put those being interviewed at their ease. Stress the importance of finding out why the accident happened so that similar events can be prevented in future. Use open questions – those that start with *what* and *how* and *why* and *who* and *where* and *when* – to encourage witnesses to talk. Use closed questions – those designed to get *yes* or *no* answers – to nail down specific matters of fact. For example, '*Was he wearing a safety helmet?*'.

  It is normally essential to write a summary of what each witness says and get them to read and sign it.

  ➤ Collect together any relevant documents, such as Permits to Work and standing orders.

- **Analyse the causes (immediate causes – basic causes - root causes)**

  ➤ The starting point for analysing an accident's causes is to ensure that the evidence is complete and consistent. Sometimes a systematic examination of the evidence will reveal the need to collect more information.

> ➤ It is common for there to be more than one cause. Sometimes it is easy to identify and treat merely the immediate causes of an accident without understanding and tackling its basic and root causes. All too often the result of doing this is another similar accident. Keep digging and asking questions until you are satisfied that you have got to the bottom of the problem.
>
> Find out whether there have been similar accidents or near misses in the past. If this accident is part of a trend, it is likely that the root cause has not been properly identified on previous occasions.

The model on the next page divides possible causes into three levels, each more important and, normally, less obvious than the one above.

- **Plan, record and implement corrective action**

  > ➤ There will often be a range of actions to take, each designed to address different causes.
  >
  > ➤ Formal accident reports are an essential part of Companies' obligations under the ISM Code to investigate accidents and near misses and implement corrective action.

- **Monitor the action taken - Follow up**

  Accident investigations can sometimes be quite time consuming. Once they are over and the necessary actions have been implemented there can be a temptation to regard the incident as closed. But of course the most important part of the entire process still remains – checking that the actions taken are being properly and consistently carried out and are, in fact, preventing similar accidents in the future.

IMMEDIATE CAUSES	
These are the easiest to spot. They are often obvious and can involve either or both of …	
Unsafe site/job conditions	**Unsafe acts by individuals**
For example, someone falls off a ladder because the handrail was loose	For example, someone gets an eye injury because of using a lathe without wearing goggles

BASIC CAUSES	
Don't stop with the immediate causes. Ask **WHY?**	
Why was the handrail broken? There could be a number of reasons. Here are typical answers to that question. *'Handrails are not included in our maintenance and inspection programme'* *'Well, it was noticed at the last safety inspection and it was on the list to get fixed. But we've been busy and we haven't got around to it yet'*	**Why** no goggles? Again, there could be many answers: • there were no goggles available at the site • lack of skill, knowledge or training; • attitude *('It's only a little job. There's no need to bother with goggles')*; • belief *('These rules are for the company's benefit. Nobody's watching. I won't get caught')*; • personality *('I like to get on with things. The occasional short cut saves time')* • emotional state *('I'm under a lot of pressure to get this job finished. I just forgot')*

ROOT CAUSES	
Once more, don't stop asking questions. Is there a failure of management control here? Are procedures inadequate? Are SMS procedures not implemented or followed up?	
For example: • What is the process for implementing and following up unsafe conditions picked up during safety inspections? • Are timescales too long? • Does the Safety Supervisor have sufficient authority to make sure that action is taken? And so on.	For example: • Who is allowed to use machinery in the workshop? • What supervision is provided? • What warnings are provided? • What precautions are specified? And so on.

Modified Accident Causation Model (Mitchell/Sagen)

2. TOOLS FOR IMPROVING SAFETY

2.0 INTRODUCTION

The previous Section of the manual described the principles of the ship's safety system. This Section covers the details of safety inspection and accident prevention in different areas and for different activities on board.

Note: You may photocopy the blank job description, the checklists and the guidance notes for use on board your ship. The contents are summarised below.

- **Accidents: Causes and Prevention**

  This is a brief general description of where accidents occur on board, who to and what can be done to prevent them.

- **A Safety Supervisor's Job Description**

  This is a blank form which those individuals with the specific role of Safety Supervisor can complete and agree with their Masters, using the guidance in Section 1 to do so in the light of their companies' policies and the circumstances on their particular ships.

- **Checklists for Safety Inspections**

  Safety inspections must be carried out systematically and consistently if they are to maintain and improve high standards of safety. It is particularly important to have an established system in place when key individuals, such as the Safety Supervisor, sign off and are replaced by others unfamiliar with the ship and its operating procedures. Checklists are a simple, powerful method for ensuring continuity.

  The following examples of checklists are provided. Modify these to suit your ship's circumstances.

  - Ship departure

  - Daily inspections

  - Galley

  - Engine Room

  - Machinery

  - Living conditions

- **Guidance notes for accident prevention**

  These consist of a series of examples covering different areas and working activities on board. They illustrate a systematic approach which can be applied to particular activities on your ship. Each example covers:

- Common accidents and injuries

- Use of protective equipment

- Actions to prevent accidents

- Space to add comments relevant to your ship

The areas covered are:

Slips and falls

Ship handling

- Mooring

- Anchoring

- Gangways

- Bridge watch duties

Cargo holds and tanks

- Winch and crane operation

- Use of trucks in cargo holds

- Working on car decks of ferries

- Tank cleaning

- Inerting of tanks and holds

- Tankers: work by/with manifolds

- Cargo hold cleaning

- Manual sounding of tanks

Engine room

- Engine room: working with oil/fuel separators

- Engine room: working with fuel injection nozzles

- Engine room: working in workshop

- Working with sanitary plants and sewage

General maintenance

- Rust removal

> Painting

> Working aloft/on scaffolding

> Use of high pressure equipment

Storage

> Handling and storage of chemicals and solvents

> Provision stores

Drills

> Abandon ship drills involving lifeboat launching

2.1   ACCIDENTS: CAUSES AND PREVENTION

The ISM Code requires Companies to *'establish safeguards against all identified risks'*. Detailed risk assessments are essential to identify risks properly, but it is also helpful for everyone on board to be aware, in general terms, of who are most likely to be involved in accidents, where they are most likely to occur and the principal ways in which they can be prevented.

2.1.1   People

There are four categories of people who are more likely to have accidents on board.

1. Young people.

2. Inexperienced crew members, particularly those who have signed on for the first time.

3. Non-professional seafarers, such as entertainers and bar staff on cruise ships.

4. Older crew members. As people get older they often find it hard to recognise or accept, say, the increasing difficulty of lifting weights which they found easy to handle in their youth.

2.1.2   Activities

Most injuries are caused by:

1. Maintenance work on deck.

2. Maintenance work in the engine room.

3. Cargo operations.

4. Anchoring and mooring operations.

5. Cleaning of tanks and holds (falls, lack of oxygen, poisonous gases).

6. Use and handling of chemicals.

7. Handling and lifting of spares and provisions.

8. Abandon ship drills involving lifeboat launching.

9. Hot work (outside the approved workshop).

10. Entrance into confined spaces.

2.1.3 Prevention

Accidents can best be prevented through:

1. Effective working procedures and instructions.

2. Methods for safeguarding equipment and machinery.

3. Guidelines for the use and maintenance of tools.

4. Thorough basic safety training, vocational training and familiarisation.

5. Active support from qualified individuals of the necessary safety management work onboard.

A SAFETY SUPERVISOR'S JOB DESCRIPTION

See Section 1, Page 7

SAFETY SUPERVISOR **Job Description**
Job purpose
Job structure
Job responsibilities

2.3 CHECKLISTS

CHECKLIST: Ship departure			
	OK	Not OK	Notes
Manning			
Health certificates valid			
Medical supplies			
Fire safety • Fire hose cabinets • Portable extinguishers serviced • Gas bottles secured			
Personnel safety equipment • Davits/lifeboats • Life rafts serviced/lashed • Life jackets located • Escape routes open • Survival suits ready • Safety stretcher ready • Alarm systems working			
Personal protective equipment • Helmets, shoes, goggles • Jackets, gloves • Safety harness • Breathing apparatuses			
Gas/oxygen meters calibrated			
Hull openings closed			
Date	**Checked by**		**Signature**

CHECKLIST: Daily inspection			
	OK	**Not OK**	**Notes**
• Gangway • Access ship/ship • Safety net • Life buoys • Guarding			
Equipment on deck • Hatch covers closed • Low recesses marked • Dangerous areas?			
Ship's deck • Portables lashed • Ropes/wires clear • Deck washed down • Walkways skid-protected • Passage marked • Ladders/rails			
Working aloft • Responsible for work • Need for work permit? • Rigging? • Safety lines with hook • Safety harness • Ships side work safety • Ladders safe • " hand support • " back support			
Confined spaces • Responsible for work? • Work permit required? • Gas measurement done? • Ventilation of • Outside guard • Risk of falls?			
Date	**Checked by**		**Signature**

CHECKLIST: Galley			
	OK	Not OK	Notes

Galley personnel
 	
• Only authorised personnel present?
 	
• If not, closed?
 	
• Qualified personnel with understanding of:
 	
   ■ Bacteria
 	
   ■ Infections
 	
   ■ damaged food
 	
   ■ nutrition
 	
   ■ special nutrition
 	
   ■ food storage
 	
• Knowledge of fire fighting			

Cleanliness • Daily cleaning rota • Hand washing facilities provided • No insects • General cleanliness			
Waste • Appropriate waste baskets • Instructions for garbage treatment			
Fire • Fire extinguisher • Fire blanket • No gas vessels			
Ventilation • Means of closing ventilation in the event of fire • Cleaning of ventilation filter			

CHECKLIST: Galley (continued)			
	OK	**Not OK**	**Notes**
• Equipment • General condition • Lighting levels • Support rails • Electrical installation totally enclosed/watertight • Confined spaces alarmed			
Storage areas • Dry provision room, sufficient shelves • Heavy items safely stored • Cleaning chemicals properly labelled/safely stored			
Risks: general • Risk of falls? • Risk of burns? • Fire risk?			
Date	**Checked by**		**Signature**

CHECKLIST: Engine room			
	OK	**Not OK**	**Notes**
Noise levels • Warning signs • Hearing protection provided? • Hearing protection worn? • Sound protected rooms effective?			
Vibrations • Vibrating parts checked • Extreme vibrations reported			
Ventilation • Appropriate • Quick closing function			
Lighting • Main lighting • Dark areas?			
Rotating machinery • Mechanical protection • Critical marked out • Exhaust pipes insulated			
Electrical plant • Main switchboard protected • Electrical tools safe			
Cranes and lifting equipment • Cranes working • Tackles working • Condition of slings			
Tanks and compartments • Hazardous tanks and compartments clearly labelled			

CHECKLIST: Engine room (continued)			
	OK	Not OK	Notes
Workshop • Eye protection provided • Eye protection used • Machine guards in place • Electrical supply safe • Tool storage • Material storage • General cleanliness			
Fire precautions • Fire detection working • Quick closing fuel working • Fire fighting cabinets ready • CO2-alarm known/OK • No gasoline in engine room • Instructions for oily waste			
Escape routes • Marked? • Open?			
Date	**Checked by**		**Signature**

CHECKLIST: Machinery			
	OK	Not OK	Notes
Emergency stop			
Prevention of accidental start (labels, signs, marking)			
Prevention of operation without guards			
Rotating parts properly guarded			
Safety pins in place for locking of gears, brakes etc on winches and capstans			
No temporary replacements of original parts			
Systems of checks in place before operation of new/repaired equipment			
Restriction of operation to properly qualified/trained personnel			
Date	**Checked by**		**Signature**

CHECKLIST: Living accommodation			
	OK	Not OK	Notes
Accommodation • Lights • Ventilation			
Cabin • Bunks • Bedclothes			
Showers and toilets			
Mess-room and recreation rooms			
Catering • Nutrition • Variety			
Welfare, recreation			
Date	**Checked by**		**Signature**

2.4 ACCIDENT PREVENTION

2.4.1 Slips and falls

Slips and falls

Injuries

Compared to many of the injuries which can be sustained while carrying out the different types of work covered in this Section of the manual, those from slips and falls (apart from falls from a height, of course) are comparatively minor.

We have put slips and falls first, however, because they are one of the largest groups of accident, accounting for about 20% of the total. And while injuries sustained are rarely severe, they can result in a temporary inability to work on board or even having to sign off.

Use of protective equipment

Appropriate footwear is an obvious defence against slips and falls. The soles of the shoes or boots for use on hard surfaces, such as steel decks, must have both shock absorbing material in the heel and a non-skid, soft sole which adapts itself to the contours of the surface.

Some companies supply seafarers with appropriate working footwear and this often conforms to a national or international standard.

However, most seafarers will change into casual shoes during their time off. That is when many slips and falls will occur, so proper footwear on its own will not solve this problem.

Preventive actions

- Reduce the likelihood of slips with:
  - Anti-skid coatings and paints
  - Non-skid mats
- Ensure that safety inspections include attention to:
  - Water penetration under tiles and flooring causing unevenness under foot
  - Oil stains and other 'housekeeping' issues for immediate correction
  - Common locations of falls and slips, such as steep staircases
- Use contrast paint to clearly mark obstacles which cannot be removed, such as doorsteps and 'stumbling blocks' on deck
- Ensure that temporary openings in the deck are fenced off
- Provide adequate lighting

Your ship

2.4.2 Ship handling

Mooring

Common accidents and injuries

- Being hit or caught by the hawser (often serious or even fatal)
- Falls and trips
- Hand injuries or bruises, especially from handling of worn-out hawsers
- Skin burns caused by nylon/polypropylene hawsers
- Back injuries caused by handling of heavy loads/pulling
- Frostbite in cold climates (note – temperature and wind chill)
- Sunstroke/sunburn in hot climates

Use of protective equipment

- Helmet
- Safety shoes
- Gloves
- Ear protectors
- Protective clothing

Preventive actions

- Agreed procedures for mooring
- Present mooring planned
- Communication signals understood
- Proper maintenance of equipment (check the safety locking pins)
- Damaged hawsers replaced
- Correct location of throwing lines
- Supporting equipment on fixed brackets
- Deck area kept clear and free of oil spill
- Mechanical protection of crew members' positions (avoid coils)
- Identify safest location for crew members
- Appropriate use of special protective clothing, depending upon weather conditions
- Protection from wind and sun covering
- Ear protection provided for maximum noise level
- Crew members involved to be properly qualified, trained and familiar with the instructions for the relevant mooring gear on the ship, such as the operation of brakes, gear and transmission functions.

Your ship

Anchoring

Common accidents and injuries:

- Falling overboard
- Being hit by hitting the anchor chain (often serious or fatal)
- Fall and trips
- Damage to the eyes by dust and mud
- Inhaling dust
- Frostbite in cold climates (note – temperature and wind chill)
- Sunstroke/sunburn in hot climates
- Damage to hearing (from free fall of the anchor)
- Injuries to upper body caused by incorrect operation of brakes and handles

Use of protective equipment:

- Goggles
- Dust mask
- Safety shoes
- Ear protectors
- Gloves

Preventive actions:

- Plan and agree communication, establish eye contact
- When using walkie-talkies, always use ship's name to avoid confusion with other ships
- Familiarise all involved with procedure and instructions
- Skid-protect the deck
- Keep deck clear from other objects, check oil spill
- Ensure appropriate lighting, have spare flashlight available
- Anchor chain to be properly marked
- Anchor gear to be well adjusted for smooth operation
- Check brake before the release of chain stopper
- Keep safe distance from chain (which may break)

Your ship

Gangways

Common accidents and injuries:

- Fall from gangway into the sea or onto the dock
- Falls and trips
- Falling between steps
- Becoming hooked in the rigging
- Back injuries during rigging and handling of gangways

Use of protective equipment

- When rigging:
  - Helmet
  - Gloves
  - Safety footwear
  - Lifeline
- When using:
  - Check and adjust for draft
- For passage:
  - Use gloves
  - Avoid carrying heavy loads

Preventive actions:

- Prepare safety net (obey the regulations for safety net rigging)
- Ensure proper lighting
- Ensure life buoy available or in vicinity
- Establish guarding arrangement (by crew or watchman)
- Prepare lightweight gangway for transfer ship-to-ship

Your ship

Bridge watch duties
Common accidents and injuries: • Back pain associated with standing position • Development, over time, of injuries caused by static working positions • Eye problems caused by continuous concentrated staring • Problems from repeated change of temperatures (inside/outside)
Use of protective equipment • Ergonomic seating with proper back support • Adjustable chart-boards
Preventive actions: • Avoid night-blinding by use of proper lighting in wheelhouse area • Alternation of duties to avoid repetitive working • Simple exercises to avoid stiffness • Frequently change working positions
Your ship

Cargo holds and tanks

Winch and crane operation
Common accidents and injuries
• Boom falling because of overload or faulty rigging
• Personnel hit by falling loads/objects
• Personnel struck while manoeuvring of cargo or loads
• Back injuries from attempting to move heavy loads manually
• Hand injuries from sharp edges etc.
Use of protective equipment
• Helmet
• Safety shoes
• Gloves
• Safety jacket with reflective material
Preventive actions
• Ensure proper lighting in working area
• Work within specified parameters for lifting equipment such as range and maximum load
• Check location and function of emergency stop and safety procedures
• Clarify standard procedures for communication and signals
• Ensure proper qualification and training of operators
• Prepare proper place for goods or provisions in advance
• Plan further transportation of goods or provisions
Your ship

Use of trucks in cargo holds

Common accidents and injuries

- Collisions with personnel working in the hold
- Damage to the ship's structure
- Damage to cargo
- Cargo caused to fall
- Individuals trapped between trucks and bulkheads
- Poisoning by truck exhaust in closed holds
- Back injuries for truck operator
- Damage to truck operators' hearing problems
- Respiratory diseases caused, over time, by inhaling exhaust fumes

Use of protective equipment

- Helmet
- Safety shoes
- Gloves
- Ear protectors
- Dust mask
- Safety jacket

Preventive actions

- Mark out the working area properly
- Plan and avoid the need for trucks to negotiate different levels
- Prevent slippery decks
- Provide appropriate lighting level
- Provide appropriate ventilation
- No other work to be done in the operating areas
- Establish and enforce the maximum number of trucks allowed
- Agree co-ordination when using several trucks
- Plan and agree max speed, and inform truck drivers
- Ensure that trucks are in proper working order, including:
  - PROPER DAMPING FACILITIES
  - FUNCTIONING WARNING LIGHTS
  - WIDE SIDE MIRRORS
- Treat goods not suited for truck transportation separately

Your ship

Working on car decks of ferries

Common accidents and injuries

- Personnel hit by car
- Individuals trapped between car and ship's structure
- Fall and trips
- Poisoning by exhaust gas
- Respiratory diseases caused, over time, by inhaling exhaust fumes

Use of protective equipment

- Helmet
- Ear protectors
- Gloves
- Safety shoes
- Safety jacket with reflective material

Preventive actions

- Establish procedures for refusing vehicles carrying dangerous goods so that they do not enter the ship
- Establish and enforce the maximum number of vehicles permitted
- Separate trucks and cars
- Clearly mark traffic lanes
- Install traffic mirrors at hidden areas
- Install well lit signs for drivers to follow
- Keep decks free from mud and dirt
- Provide car grip or skid protection on decks
- Have procedures for lashing of non-standard vehicles
- Ensure appropriate ventilation
- Use combined ear protectors and communication equipment
- Agree who is in charge of operational decisions
- Provide sufficient personnel for directing vehicles on and off the ship
- Ensure that personnel spend as little time as possible on the car deck
- Ensure that all relevant personnel receive prior training and preparation

Your ship

Tank cleaning

Common accidents and injuries

- Explosion
- Gas poisoning or lack of oxygen
- Serious falls
- Claustrophobia
- Injuries caused by handling heavy equipment
- Long term effects of inhaling poisonous gases

Use of protective equipment

- Helmet
- Goggles/Visor
- Gloves for chemical handling
- Safety footwear
- Appropriate protecting clothing
- Appropriate breathing apparatus/filter masks

Preventive actions

- Permit to Work system enforced
- Examine general procedures; plan for specific tasks
- Establish procedures for the handling of sediment
- Verify that all personnel are familiar with tank cleaning procedures
- Prepare first aid possibilities (eye-washing, etc.)
- Prepare for the use of showers
- Establish regular drills of emergency procedures
- Check the last 3 cargoes for poisonous gas content (H2S, etc)
- Gas and oxygen measurement to be done by qualified person
- Continuous gas measurement/personal gas/oxygen warning kit
- Continuous oxygen measurement/personal gas/oxygen warning kit
- Maintain gas instrument calibration (two sets required for tankers)
- Walkie-talkie for communication with bridge/responsible person
- Fire alert, as per procedural requirement
- Watchman outside entrance, safety lines, portable fire extinguisher
- Ensure appropriate ventilation, in accordance with tank design
- Provide sufficient lighting
- Check and confirm condition of entrance hatch/ladders
- Use internal ladders for personnel movement only (No extra loads)
- Divide stay in tank into short time periods

Your ship

Inerting of tanks and holds

Common accidents and injuries

- Death from asphyxiation - inert gas is extremely dangerous!
- Preliminary symptoms by inhaling of inert gas: dizziness, discomfort, disorientation

Use of protective equipment

- Same procedures as for working in any gaseous atmosphere onboard

Preventive actions

- Follow procedures/instructions for the operation of inert gas plants
- For technical procedures, production plant, maintenance etc. always refer to makers' instructions and regulations
- Ensure appropriate ventilation in any closed compartment where inert gas equipment is installed
- Ensure that all accesses to inerted tanks or holds are carefully closed
- Provide warnings against any movement in areas where inert gas is exhausted
- Always be at the "windward side" of inert gas equipment
- Prevent anyone entering any inerted room or compartment without proper breathing equipment and all associated safety precautions.

Your ship

Tankers: Work by/with manifold

Common accidents and injuries

- Fire and explosions
- Gas poisoning and asphyxiation from lack of oxygen
- Skin damage by caustic agents, spraying or flushing
- Falls caused by leakage, in particular around oil trough
- Eczema, eye and lung diseases
- Back or body injuries caused by handling of heavy hoses and equipment
- Long term diseases caused by inhaling harmful gases

Use of protective equipment

- Helmet
- Goggles/visor
- Safety footwear
- Chemically resistant gloves
- Overalls or protective suits if required
- Walkie-talkie

Preventive actions

- Prepare datasheets for hazardous cargo content or relevant cargo information in order to identify adequate protective aids required
- Establish and enforce special precautions for cargo with a high content of H2S (hydrogen sulphide)
- Prepare suitable manning for relevant operations
- Provide correct lifting gear for hoses and equipment
- Skid protect decks; have sawdust or powder available
- Safeguard openings
- Provide proper lighting
- Prepare appropriate and properly maintained tools
- Keep working areas tidy (no storing here)
- Plan, prepare and mark which manifold to be operated
- Ensure no pressure in the deck pipes before any opening
- Keep distance before pressurising of the system

Your ship

Cargo hold cleaning

Common accidents and injuries

- Dust explosion
- Poisoning caused by dangerous cargo contamination
- Dizziness and disorientation, especially in small/deep rooms
- Lung diseases caused by dust particles, etc.
- Eye infections
- Allergy and skin infections
- Long-time effects from inhaling of dust and vapours

Use of protective equipment

- Helmet
- Goggles
- Gloves
- Safety footwear
- Overall
- Appropriate filter mask the cargo (check work instruction)

Preventive actions

- Adequate ventilation
- Adequate lighting, including possible additional portable lighting in the holds
- Effective water-jets or vacuum cleaning (Minimise manual handling)
- Mechanise traditional heavy work for the removal of cargo remains
- Plan and prepare best cleaning procedure depending on cargo condition
- Station supervisor/watchman on deck during hold cleaning
- Ensure dedicated procedures for the particular ship (not general)

Your ship

Manual soundings of tanks
Common accidents and injuries • Sick and dizzy, caused by oily fumes • Risk of fire • Skin problems, caused by skin contact with oily agents • Breathing problems, caused by inhaling of oily fumes
Use of protective equipment • Helmet • Safety footwear • Chemical resistant gloves • Eye goggles • Half-mask with dedicated/approved filter (A2/P2)
Preventive actions • Cleanliness in the sounding area • Sounding equipment to be cleaned when sounding is finished • Avoid skin contact with oily agents • Ensure proper hand hygiene, use protective cream • Ensure that the sounding pipe is properly closed
Your ship

Engine room

Working with oil/fuel separators
Common accidents and injuries • Sickness and dizzyness from oil fumes • Skin irritation caused by chemicals • Eczema and oil allergy • Long term effects: asthma or other diseases
Use of protective equipment • Helmet • Eye protection • Chemical resistant gloves • Safety footwear • Breathing protection, such as face mask with approved filter (A2, P2 etc.)
Preventive actions • Establish and follow written work procedures • Ensure that those involved are certified as qualified by a responsible person – self-teaching of procedures and instructions will not do! • Plan and schedule the work correctly • Check makers' instruction/recommendation for working with separators • Use specially designed lifting gear for mounting/dismounting of centrifuge • Provide supporting sketches and drawings at the site • Agree lifting arrangements to avoid inconvenient manual lifting. • Use special tools for mounting/dismounting of separator • Ensure ample cooling period before work starts • Provide good ventilation/exhaust fans when dismantling • Close the connection to other systems to avoid back-blows
Your ship

Working with fuel injection nozzles

Common accidents and injuries

- Eye problems caused by spraying
- Lung damage caused by oil fumes (aerosols). This may lead to pneumonia.
- Long term diseases of the lung from the same cause
- Fire

Use of protective equipment

- Helmet
- Safety footwear
- Goggles/visor
- Filter mask with filter (A2/P2)

Preventive actions

- Discuss and agree proper procedures
- Arrange workplace so that face and eyes are protected
- Design workplace as a "box" with a glass window in front
- Provide a local exhaust fan
- Avoid splashing and fumes
- Provide appropriate ventilation in the room
- Carry out testing operations in another compartment
- Absolutely no smoking!

Your ship

Working in engine-room workshop

Common accidents and injuries

- Minor and serious cuts and wounds
- Back and shoulder injuries caused by heavy lifting
- Muscular problems caused by poor ergonomics
- Eye injuries from by grinding and other metal work
- Hearing loss caused by high noise levels
- Dehydration caused by high temperatures (in tropic zones)

Use of protective equipment

- Goggles or other appropriate eye protection
- Gloves
- Safety shoes
- Ear protectors
- Equipment for lifting and moving heavy objects
- Appropriate chairs and footstools for different working positions

Preventive actions

- Do the work in well ventilated or air-conditioned rooms
- Provide portable working lamps
- Provide goggles beside the workplaces at which they will be needed
- Frequent check the balance of grinding wheels
- Systematically plan large maintenance tasks
- Store dedicated workshop tools systematically
- Frequently check the condition of tools. Repair or replace as necessary
- Do not disconnect fire detectors for welding work – use a watchman
- Identify and provide any special requirements for welding in workshop/engine room

Your ship

Working with sanitary plants and sewage

Common accidents and injuries

- Scratches and cuts on the hands
- Serious infection of cuts and scratches
- Risk for several serious diseases, such as tetanus and hepatitis A
- Infection in breathing organs, caused by bacterial infections
- Problems caused by use of chemicals

Use of protective equipment

- Gloves (extra long)
- Safety footwear
- Filter mask
- Overalls
- Suitable tools to avoid the use of hands inside pipes and tanks
- Means of quickly disinfecting scratches and cuts

Preventive actions

- Vaccination, in particular for tetanus and hepatitis A
- Appropriate cleaning facilities for clothes and equipment
- Plan the work to avoid direct contact with sewage
- Use system drawings before dismantling to prevent static pressure
- Be aware of the risks from poisonous gases
- Inform relevant responsible person
- Avoid the use of pressurised air for unblocking pipes (splashing)
- Be aware of special instructions for passenger ships as they have comprehensive sewage processing plants with restricted outlets

Your ship

Rust removal

Common accidents and injuries

- Eye injury caused by rust particles and dust
- Cut and bruises on hands, which may become infected
- Long term effects, caused by inhaling dust
- Muscular injuries from working in inconvenient positions
- Serious falls from scaffoldings etc
- 'White fingers' (blood circulation), caused by the use of vibrating tools

Use of protective equipment

- Helmet
- Safety footwear
- Gloves
- Goggles
- Filter mask (min. P2 filter)
- Knee/foot protection or special foundation for 'knee working position'

Preventive actions

- Agree procedures for working hours and change of duties
- Plan the work to avoid long periods of rust removal
- Prepare the workplace to minimise lifting and moving
- Use tools with low vibration and low noise levels
- Permits to Work in certain hazardous areas (e.g. if there is a risk of fire)
- Use supports to improve the working position

'White finger'

EU directives require that the level of vibration has to be marked on the tools.
Basic guidelines to avoid 'white fingers' from the use of vibrating tools are as follows:

Vibration level	Max effective working hour per day
140 dB (HA)	0.5 hour
135 dB (HA)	1 hour
130 dB (HA)	4 hours
125 dB (HA)	Limited risk

Your ship

Painting

Common accidents and injuries

- Risk of explosion and fire
- Poisoning by paint solvents
- Irritation of eyes, skin and breathing organs
- Blood poisoning through skin bruises and high pressure painting
- Development of allergies
- Long term illnesses from exposure to solvents
- Muscular injuries from working in inconvenient positions
- Serious fall when working aloft

Use of protective equipment

- Helmet
- Safety shoes
- Gloves
- Goggles
- Filter mask

For high pressure painting, see 'Use of high pressure equipment' below

Preventive actions

- By the Company:
  - Clear recommendations and instructions for types of paint to be used for different jobs
  - Clear highlighting of the risks of different types of paint. For example 'Very poisonous', 'Poisonous', 'Caustic', 'Corrosive', 'Harmful', 'Less harmful'
- By the ship:
  - If possible, avoid the use of dangerous paint with a low code number
  - Do not choose a particular type of paint without checking the instructions for use issued by the Company
  - Ensure that everyone involved understands the paint code system, warning labels and signs etc, together with the written procedures for painting
  - Provide adequate lighting and ventilation in the paint shop
  - Provide a separate area in the paint shop for mixing and preparation
  - Check that the paint shop contains a working fire extinguisher
  - Ensure that any scaffolding or rigging used is properly erected
  - Close the area to be painted to those not involved
  - Properly ventilate closed compartments
  - If possible, avoid high pressure painting

Your ship

Working aloft/overside/on scaffolding

Common accidents and injuries

- Falls resulting in serious injuries
- Drowning by falling into the sea
- Being struck by falling scaffolding or equipment
- Muscular injuries from working in inconvenient positions

Use of protective equipment

- Helmet
- Protective footwear
- Gloves
- Goggles
- Appropriate clothing
- Life line or harness, depending on the circumstances
    - Lifelines for working aloft should be no longer than 1.5–2 meters, since a fall involving a longer line can result in injury
    - Lifelines for working overside should be long enough to allow the worker to fall gently into the water and take up an appropriate swimming position while waiting for assistance to pull him from the water. The line must be fixed to a point which the rescue team can get at without difficulty.
- Life jacket, depending on the circumstances

Preventive actions

- Do as much of the work aloft or requiring scaffolding as possible during shipyard docking
- Never carry out work overside while underway
- Establish and enforce clear written procedures for working on scaffolding and aloft
- Use only approved scaffolding
- Ensure that those carrying out the work are properly trained
- Do not allow those who suffer from vertigo to work on scaffolding or aloft
- If necessary, use Permits to Work
- Thoroughly inspect the work before starting
- Repeat the inspection before changing position
- Plan the movement of scaffolding and equipment
- Provide continuous of the work
- Agree methods of communication

Your ship

Use of high pressure equipment

Common accidents and injuries

- Bruising and cuts

- Eye injuries

- Breathing problems from inhaling dust

- **Note:** The use of ultra-high pressure equipment (above 150 bars) is extremely dangerous and can cause serious injuries.

Use of protective equipment

- Helmet

- Visor

- Gloves

- Safety footwear

- Working overalls

- Breathing apparatuses or filter mask of relevant category

- Normal protective clothing is not sufficient when using ultra-high pressure equipment. Operators must use special suits, approved for the relevant working pressure.

Preventive actions

- Heavy equipment should have supporting racks/brackets

- Trigger handle must not be of the locking type

- Ensure effective ventilation/breathing means for sand-blasting

- Check that hoses are certified for relevant working pressure

- Feeding lines to be permanently installed (steel pipes)

- Check proper installation and function of compressor filters

Your ship

2.4.6 **Storage**

Note: Please refer to your national regulations covering the storage and use of substances injurious to health onboard. This guidance note is only a short general reminder of the main topics:

Storage and handling of chemicals and solvents

Common accidents and injuries

- Short term effects include irritation of the skin, dizzyness, sickness, headache, disorientation and feeling 'drunk'

- Diseases caused by contact with skin, eyes, etc.

- Inhaling dust, vapour, gases, etc.

- Serious long term effects can include cancer and damage to the brain and central nervous system

Use of protective equipment

- It is not possible to generalise about the protective equipment needed for the safe handling of chemicals and solvents. Not only are some substances more dangerous than others, different substances affect human beings in very different ways. It is therefore very important to check the documentation for each substance and follow the instructions precisely. If for any reason the documentation is missing or difficult to understand, do not proceed. Seek help from your shore based office.

Preventive actions

- **Note:** The most effective method of protection against possible damage from dangerous chemicals is not to use them! While that will not always be possible, all of those involved, both at Company level and on each ship, should work to minimise their use and establish clear procedures for when they have to be used.

- Secure chemicals in store to remove any danger of spillage

- Store chemicals only in their original boxes and cans, properly labelled

- Do not accept incorrectly labelled chemicals

- Labelling must make clear:
    - ANY POISONOUS EFFECTS
    - RISKS OF FIRE OR EXPLOSION
    - INSTRUCTION FOR FIRST AID IN THE EVENT OF AN ACCIDENT
    - REQUIRED STORAGE TEMPERATURE, IF ANY

- Keep data-sheets in the store room for all chemicals

- Keep the chemical store locked, with access under the control of a named responsible person

- Establish a detailed record of the use of chemicals, kept up to date by the responsible person

- Only allow qualified individuals, who understand the data on the labels, including procedures for first aid, to work with dangerous chemicals

---

- When using chemicals:
  - Follow established procedures
  - Arrange 'closed systems', avoiding direct contact with chemicals
  - If this is not possible, use methods which minimise direct contact
  - Ensure proper ventilation of the workplace
  - Prepare no more than the quantity of chemical required
  - Avoid heavy cans, which are difficult to handle
  - Know the location of the medical cabinet in case of accidents

Your ship

Provision stores

Common accidents and injuries

- Being hit by falling objects
- Injuries from the incorrect use of handling gear
- Cut from broken glass, sharp edges etc.
- Back injuries caused by heavy lifting

Use of protective equipment

- Helmet
- Safety footwear
- Gloves
- Appropriate clothing for different temperature zones

Preventive actions

- Organise the store layout so that:
  - The most frequently used provisions are the easiest to get at
  - Shelf heights are appropriate for both light and heavy goods, to avoid the need for heavy lifting
  - There is adequate permanent lighting and additional portable lighting if necessary.
- Provide the appropriate tools, which may include:
  - Simple mechanical handling equipment so that provisions can be moved both horizontally and vertically within the store with a minimum of manual handling
  - Roll wagons with brake
  - Small electrically driven trucks
  - Footstools, portable ladders, etc
  - Tools for opening boxes and packages (to save hands)
- Stow provisions safely and efficiently by:
  - Arranging for sufficient manning (this is not a one man job!)
  - Considering unpacking some goods on the quay
  - Planning the sequence of stowage to avoid blocking
  - Checking that shore or shipboard cranes offer convenient access
  - Ensuring that nothing is stowed above 1.5 metres
- Work safely and efficiently by:
  - Ensuring that all operators receive training in safe lifting
- Whenever possible, using mechanical equipment to avoid manual handling of goods

Your ship

Abandon ship drills involving lifeboat launching

Common accidents and injuries

- Serious, or even fatal injuries from the accidental release of hooks
- Injury to the head and body from being thrown against the ship
- Trapped limbs
- Falling into the sea

Use of protective equipment

- Life jacket
- Helmet
- Protective footwear
- Gloves
- Appropriate clothing

Preventive actions

- During SOLAS drill launching it is specified that the lifeboat is launched with **assigned lifeboat operating crew only**. All members of assigned crews must have lifeboat competence certificates. The remainder of the lifeboat's complement can then enter the boat after launching to complete the drill.
- Ensure that all crewmembers are fully familiarised with their duties and assigned lifeboat stations
- Ensure sufficient free place at the embarkation deck and safeguard the station using rails, etc.
- Consider the possible use of lifelines
- Check that access to the embarkation station is free of obstacles
- Ensure regular maintenance, in accordance with the maker's instruction manual, of:
  - Davits
  - Lashing equipment
  - Operational gears
  - Safety arrangements
  - Wire etc.
- When the drill is finished, check proper lashing and protection

Your ship

3. HEALTH ON BOARD

3.0 INTRODUCTION

This section of the manual contains:

- **A fit and healthy crew?**

  Medical examinations and certificates for crew joining the ship.

- **Be prepared!**

  - ➢ Medical supplies

  - ➢ Medical training

  - ➢ Requesting assistance from shore based medical personnel

- **General health protection on board**

  - ➢ Manual handling

  - ➢ Personal protective equipment

  - ➢ Stress

- **Hygiene**

  - ➢ Cleanliness on board

  - ➢ Food storage and preparation

- **Substances hazardous to health**

  - ➢ Solvents and other harmful chemicals

  - ➢ Asbestos

- **Infectious diseases and malaria**

3.1 A FIT AND HEALTHY CREW?

The ISM Code says that:

*The Company should ensure that each ship is manned with qualified, certificated **and medically fit** seafarers in accordance with national and international requirements* (The emphasis is our own).

To make sure that companies meet this requirement, each administration has slightly different regulations and recommendations covering pre-employment, return to work after sickness and regular medical examinations.

A useful source of general guidance is 'Guidelines for conducting pre-sea and periodic medical fitness examinations for seafarers', published jointly by the International Labour Office (ILO) and the World Health Organisation (WHO).

Obviously pre-employment medical examinations are conducted ashore and are therefore not the ship's responsibility. ***But:***

- You must have a system for checking that new members of the crew have the proper medical certificates on joining.

- Be aware that certain administrations only permit approved doctors to carry out these medical examinations. If a seafarer attempts to join your ship without having had the correct examination you may find that the nearest approved doctor is a long way from where the ship is docked.

3.2 BE PREPARED

3.2.1 Medical supplies and equipment

All ships must have a medicine cabinet or chest onboard. The medical supplies which it contains will be specified by your administration (for example, EU directive 92/29/EEC/1992). The contents will be required to be checked regularly (annually in many cases) by an approved doctor or pharmacist.

3.2.2 Medical training

It is a requirement that ships' Masters and Chief Officers should have an acceptable knowledge of first aid and basic medical training.

In addition, the ship must be equipped with a suitable medical handbook for ships, approved by the administration. Examples include:

- British Red Cross: 'First Aid Manual'

- World Health Organisation: 'International Medical Guide for Ships'

Requesting assistance from shore based medical personnel

There are occasions when illness or injury on board will be beyond the capabilities of senior officers to deal with using their knowledge of first aid and basic medical training. Help will need to be sought, in the first instance, by contacting shore based medical personnel. Most seafaring countries have set up arrangements for doing so. These include standard checklists of information which ships must have available to help medical personnel ashore diagnose the problem and suggest treatment.

For example, all member states of the European Union are responsible for maintaining a medical service centre for ships and seafarers. When medical emergencies arise, each ship must be able to supply the centres with the following information:

Patient's details

- Date of birth
- Position onboard

The ship

- Position or fishing-place
- Destination

The problem

- Description
- How long has the problem been present?
- How did the problem start?
- Where is the problem located?
- Is this the first time the problem has occurred?

Vital signs

- Is the patient conscious?
- Can the patient breathe normally?
- What is the patient's heart rate?
- What is the patient's temperature?

Medical history

- Is the patient currently receiving any kind of medication or other medical treatment?
- Does the patient have any allergies, including to any medicine?
- Has the patient previously suffered from any serious disease or illness?
- Does the patient smoke?
- Does the patient use alcohol or drugs?

GENERAL HEALTH PROTECTION ON BOARD

3.3.1   ## Manual handling

Manual handling is a common source of injury on board. Torn muscles and strained backs may not be the most serious injuries which seafarers can sustain, but they are unpleasant and can prevent individuals from working for some considerable time. If they are not properly corrected or given insufficient time to heal, permanent damage can be done which in extreme cases may involve seafarers having to give up their jobs.

Fortunately, injuries from manual handling can be avoided in two ways:

- **Don't handle heavy items manually!**

  When faced with the need to lift or move a heavy item the first question to ask is *'what mechanical means are available to help me do this?'*. Resist the temptation to 'save time' by trying to do the job manually rather than, say, going to fetch a handtruck.

- **Use proper lifting techniques**

  If manual handling cannot be avoided and the item to be moved is within the capabilities of the individual or individuals involved, injury can be avoided by using the correct technique. Here is a summary of these techniques from **'Getting to grips with manual handling'** reproduced here with the kind permission of the publishers, the United Kingdom's Health and Safety Executive.

Good handling technique

Here are some important points, using a basic lifting operation as an example.

Stop and think

Plan the lift. Where is the load to be placed? Use appropriate handling aids if possible. Do you need help with the load? Remove obstructions such as discarded wrapping materials. For a long lift, such as floor to shoulder height, consider resting the load mid-way on a table or a bench to change grip.

Position the feet

Feet apart, giving a balanced and stable base for lifting (tight skirts and unsuitable footwear make this difficult). Leading leg as far forward as is comfortable and if possible, pointing in the direction you intend to go.

Adopt a good posture

When lifting from a low level, bend the knees. But do not kneel or overflex the knees. Keep the back straight, maintaining its natural curve (tucking in the chin helps). Lean forward a little over the load if necessary to get a good grip. Keep the shoulders level and facing in the same direction as the hips.

Get a firm grip

Try to keep the arms within the boundary formed by the legs. The best position and type of grip depends on the circumstances and individual preference; but must be secure. A hook grip is less tiring than keeping the fingers straight. If you need to vary the grip as the lift proceeds, do it as smoothly as possible.

Keep close to the load

Keep the load close to the trunk for as long as possible. Keep heaviest side of the load next to the trunk. If a close approach to the load is not possible, slide it towards you before trying to lift.

Don't jerk

Lift smoothly raising the chin as the lift begins, keeping control of the load.

Move the feet

Don't twist the trunk when turning to the side.

Put down, *then* adjust

If precise positioning of the load is necessary, put it down first, then slide it into the desired position.

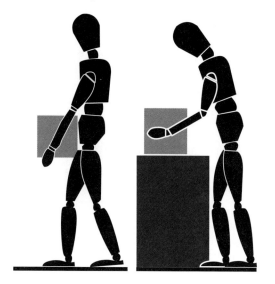

How do I know if there's a risk of injury

It's a matter of judgement in each case, but there are certain things to look out for, such as people puffing and sweating, excessive fatigue, bad posture, cramped work areas, awkward or heavy loads or a history of back troubles. Operators can often highlight which activities are unpopular, difficult or arduous.

Can you be more definite?

There is no such thing as a completely 'safe' manual handling operation. It's difficult to be precise: so many factors vary between jobs, workplaces and people. But the general risk assessment guidelines filter opposite should help to identify when a more detailed risk assessment is necessary. Working within the guidelines will reduce the need for a more detailed risk assessment.

General risk assessment guidelines

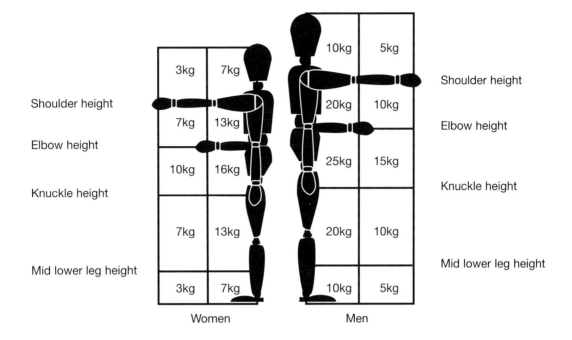

Women | Men

- Each box in the diagram above shows guideline weights for lifting and lowering.

- Observe the activity and compare to the diagram. If the lifter's hands enter more than one box during the operation, use the smallest weight. Use an in-between weight if the hands are close to a boundary between boxes. If the operation must take place with the hands beyond the boxes, make a more detail assessment.

- The weights assume that the load is readily grasped with both hands.

- The operation takes place in reasonable working conditions with the lifter in a stable body position.

- Any operation involving more than twice the guideline weights should be rigorously assessed – even for very fit, well-trained individuals working under favourable conditions.

- There is no such thing as a completely 'safe' manual handling operation. But working within the guidelines will cut the risk and reduce the need for a more detailed assessment.

81

Twisting

Reduce the guideline weights if the lifter
twists to the side during the operation.
As a rough guide, reduce them by 10%
if the handler twists beyond 45°, and by
20% if the handler twists beyond 90°.

Frequent lifting and lowering

The guideline weights are for infrequent
operations – up to about 30 operations
per hour – where the pace of work is not
forced, adequate pauses to rest or use
different muscles are possible, and the load
is not supported for any length of time.
Reduce the weights if the operation is
repeated more often. As a rough guide,
reduce the weights by 30% if the operation
is repeated five to eight times a minute; and
by 80% where the operation is repeated
more than 12 times a minute.

Are you saying I mustn't exceed the guidelines

No. The risk assessment guidelines are not
safe limits for lifting. But work outside the
guidelines is likely to increase the risk of
injury, so you should examine it closely
for possible improvements. You should
remember that you must make the work
less demanding if it's reasonably practicable
to do so.

3.3.2 Personal protective equipment

The protection of individuals from injury on board is a two way process.

- **The company** has an obligation, which in some administrations is backed by law, to:

  ➢ provide appropriate protective equipment

  ➢ train individuals where, when and how to use it

  ➢ ensure that it is properly used by effective supervision, clear working procedures and appropriate safety signs and posters.

- **Individuals** have a duty, again sometimes backed by law, to take proper care of themselves and their fellow seafarers.

The different types of personal protective equipment are summarised in the table below. This is from the United Kingdom's Maritime and Coastguard Agency's Code of Safe Working Practices for Seafarers.

Type	Examples
Head protection	Safety helmets, bump caps, hair protection
Hearing protection	Ear muffs, ear plugs
Face and eye protection	Goggles and spectacles, facial shields
Respiratory protective equipment	Dust masks, respirators, breathing apparatus
Hand and foot protection	Gloves, safety boots and shoes
Body protection	Safety suits, safety belts, harnesses, aprons, high visibility clothing
Protection against drowning	Lifejackets, buoyancy aids and lifebuoys
Protection against hypothermia	Immersion suits and anti-exposure suits

3.3.3 Stress

- **What is stress?**

  Stress is a condition experienced by individuals as a result of a combination of external and internal factors. Pressures from outside, such as work or family problems, are experienced by different individuals in different ways because of their different ages, length and type of service, personalities and so on. A relaxed, experienced Chief Officer may hardly notice a situation which would cause a high degree of anxiety in a nervous, inexperienced cadet.

  Stress creates a feeling of need to 'do something' about the situation which is causing it. Of course that 'something' may be helpful or unhelpful. One officer may handle the pressure of getting a ship ready to sail against a tight deadline by establishing clear priorities, organising his time efficiently, delegating and so on. Another may simply crack up.

The trick to managing stress is not to avoid it – since that is often neither possible nor even, in many cases, desirable. It is to learn how to cope effectively.

- **Common causes of stress at sea**

  ➤ **There's no escape!** Life for many seafarers involves spending quite long periods of time, in confined conditions, with a group of people they would not necessarily choose as friends!

  ➤ **Isolation.** Being away from home and family for a long time creates pressure, particularly if there are problems ashore.

  ➤ **Watch patterns.** Those who work shifts of any sort, whether ashore or afloat, are more likely to suffer from stress related illnesses than those who do not.

  ➤ **Heavy workloads.** These can sometimes be self imposed, particularly since those who work on board ships are not able, unlike their colleagues ashore, to 'shut the office door and go home'.

  ➤ **Boredom.** It is not always frantic work situations and crises that cause stress. Endless routine and not have enough stimulating work to do can also be a cause.

- **Symptoms of failing to cope effectively with stress**

  Stress often shows up:

  ➤ **As different sorts of illness.** Often these are comparatively minor, such as headaches, loss of appetite, coughs, muscular aches and pains, heartburn and indigestion, diarrhoea, tiredness, inability to sleep properly and so on. Unfortunately, if the underlying cause is not identified and corrected, more serious problems such as heart attacks can result.

  ➤ **As anti-social behaviour.** When people are failing to cope effectively with stress they frequently lose their sense of humour and become aggressive and uncommunicative with their colleagues.

- **Coping with stress: a healthy lifestyle on board**

  The strategies for coping effectively with stress on board are much the same as those which work ashore, though of course there are certain activities, such as going for a nice long walk in the countryside, which are not available.

  ➤ **Exercise.** Regular exercise is not simply good for the body. It also benefits the mind.

➢ **Regular sleep.** Exhaustion lowers our resistance to illness and makes it more difficult to maintain the mental sharpness, objectivity and balance which we need when faced with stressful situations.

➢ **Regular, healthy meals.** As with exercise, a sensible diet keeps the mind fit as well as the body.

➢ **Sensible use of stimulants.** If possible, avoid tobacco entirely. Aside from the considerable long term dangers to health posed by smoking, using cigarettes as a treatment for stress simply does not work.

Moderate use of alcohol is not harmful, but be careful about developing bad habits. Avoid drinking alone or heading straight for the bar at the end of a watch. Have a shower, change and relax first. Alcohol is for the heightened enjoyment of social occasions. It should not be used as an anaesthetic!

➢ **Interests outside of work.** Hobbies, reading, TV, chess – anything in fact which is not directly connected with the day to day work of being a seafarer all helps to provide something else to think about and put problems in perspective.

3.4 HYGIENE

3.4.1 Cleanliness

General cleanliness on board, coupled with high standards of personal hygiene, are amongst the most important defences against ill health at sea. When groups of people live together in the compact conditions found on board most ships, dirt and disease go hand in hand.

As with so many other aspects of safety and health, it is the responsibility of all members of the crew to maintain high standards of cleanliness, both for themselves and in their living and working environment.

3.4.2 Food

The storage, preparation and handling of food poses obvious potential dangers on board. The safe management of work in the galley requires standards and procedures for, in particular:

• Training of galley staff

• Galley equipment

• Tools, utensils, crockery, cutlery etc.

• Food storage and preparation

• Hygienic working practices

- **Training**

  All crew members who work in the galley should have received basic training in food hygiene before taking up their duties. If at all possible they should be in possession of a recognised, assessed certificate of food hygiene, such as that issued by the UK's Chartered Institute of Environmental Health.

- **Galley equipment**

  There should be a detailed procedure and rota for cleaning all galley equipment, such as stoves and refrigerators. This should specify precisely what is to be cleaned on a daily, weekly, bi-weekly and monthly basis, together with the cleaning methods and materials to be used.

- **Tools, utensils, crockery, cutlery, etc.**

  All implements used for the preparation and consumption of food must be cleaned as soon as possible after use. Dirty dishes and utensils are a prime breeding ground for bacteria. Dishwashing machines are more effective than hand washing, since they operate at much higher temperatures. Damaged implements must be discarded.

- **Food storage and preparation**

  This is a very big subject and the all important details will depend on the circumstances of your particular ship. However there are some important principles:

  > **Storage.** All food must be stored in areas which are clean, dry, at the appropriate temperature and protected from vermin and insects.

  > **NOTE: Chemicals and detergents must never be placed or stored above food (US Public Health requirement).**

  > **Segregation.** Raw food must be kept separate from cooked. Work surfaces, chopping boards and implements used for preparing meat must be separated from those used for all other foods. Frozen food must not be de-frosted in close proximity to other food. There should be separate facilities for washing food, washing hands and washing equipment used for cleaning. Cleaning materials should be stored in areas separate from those used for food storage and preparation.

  > **Temperatures.** The bacteria which cause food poisoning thrive in warm temperatures. Wherever possible food should either be piping hot or refrigerated. Once frozen food has been defrosted it should not be re-frozen.

  > **Contamination.** Food which comes in contact with damaged crockery or utensils should be discarded. Galley staff must thoroughly wash their hands after handling raw food, particularly meat and fish, before handling other types of food. Equipment which is used for different foods must be thoroughly cleaned between each use.

➢ **Waste.** Galley waste is a particularly potent source of the bacteria which cause disease. It must be kept properly contained and entirely separate from foodstuffs. It must also, of course, be disposed of in accordance with national and international regulations.

- **Hygienic working practices**

Here is a typical set of hygienic working practices for galley staff. They should be trained in its use, the list should be prominently displayed in the galley and adherence to it should be checked during regular safety inspections.

- Keep yourself clean and always wear clean clothing

- Always wear the protective clothing provided

- Always wash your hands thoroughly with hot water and soap:
  ➢ before handling food
  ➢ after using the toilet
  ➢ after touching your hair
  ➢ after handling raw foods or waste
  ➢ before starting work
  ➢ after every break
  ➢ after blowing your nose

- Do not report for work in the galley if you are suffering from diarrhoea and/or vomiting. You must obtain medical clearance before reporting for such work again.

- Report all illnesses immediately, particularly those involving rashes and spots.

- Report any cuts, however small, immediately and obtain first aid. Untreated cuts are a source of infection.

- Ensure cuts and sores are covered with a waterproof, high visibility dressing.

- Do not smoke in food storage areas, the galley or when serving food.

- Never cough or sneeze over food.

- Clean as you go. Keep all equipment and surfaces clean.

- Follow all food safety instructions on food packaging.

3.5   SUBSTANCES HAZARDOUS TO HEALTH

3.5.1   Solvents and other harmful chemicals

- **A forgotten problem?**

It is more than ten years since injuries and illness caused by solvents became widely publicised. The principal problem identified was the widespread use of trichlorethylene (Tri), a solvent which was regarded at one time as a miracle agent for many purposes on board, from washing clothes to deep cleaning of machine parts.

Because of the focus on this particular chemical there has perhaps been a tendency to think that solvent injuries were caused by our previous lack of understanding and that now we are better informed the problem has been solved and can be forgotten. Unfortunately this is not true. Serious health problems are also occurring from the improper use of modern solvents.

- **Injury and illness**

Solvents can create both short term injury and long term illness. Contact can cause rashes, burns and skin diseases. Fumes can cause breathing problems. Sometimes these are minor and disappear quite quickly. However, the effects may remain in the body and be reinforced each time the individual is exposed to the solvent. This can result in serious illness many years after exposure - even years after the seafarer has stopped sailing. Even solvents which have no apparent effect when being used can cause serious long term problems.

Note: Smoking combined with exposure to solvents increases the risk of illness.

- **Use of solvents and other dangerous chemicals: principles**

There are four basic principles governing the use of solvents and other dangerous chemicals on board. These are often covered by regulations laid down by national administrations. They are:

➤ Labelling and information

➤ A ban on the handling of especially harmful substances

➤ Training

➤ Protective measures during use.

- **Labelling and information**

All chemicals purchased for use on board must be labelled in a proper manner. The following information must be provided:

➤ Hazard classification and the symbol for health hazard/danger of fire and explosion

➤ Technical name, name of substance/product with indication of contents (harmful components)

➤ Warning of hazards and necessary precautions

➤ Name and address of producer.

No solvents, paints or other chemicals for use on board should be accepted unless this information can be clearly identified.

- **A ban on the handling of especially harmful substances**

  There must be a clearly identified list of substances which may not, under any circumstances, be handled by seafarers on board.

- **Training**

  It is essential that every individual who may be exposed to solvents and other substances hazardous to health in the course of their work on board should be clear about the dangers posed by the substances they use, how they should be handled and how to protect themselves from harm.

  It is particularly important that they understand that these substances can cause major illness long after exposure. Minor rashes and temporary dizziness may not seem too serious at the time, but they can be the first step on the road to lung cancer and premature death!

- **Protective measures during use**

  Instructions in the use of solvents and other harmful chemicals, including recommendations for protective equipment and clothing, must be followed precisely. It is sometimes easy for users to think that '*it doesn't really matter – the job will soon be done*'. Twenty years later they will regret taking this attitude, but by then it will be too late.

  Assessment of the safe use of solvents and other harmful substances should form part of regular safety inspections.

- **Records and controls**

  Accurate, up to date records will help to minimise the risks of using solvents and other harmful chemicals and should prevent improperly labelled substances being accepted on board. In particular:

  ➤ **Substance file.** There should be a substance file and product data sheet for every chemical used on board.

  ➤ **Chemicals journal.** A journal should be kept of purchases, storage conditions and quantities of harmful substances. It should also provide a record of use, documenting users' awareness of the health risks and necessary precautions.

  Systematic use of such a journal will lead to greater awareness of the dangers involved and, in many cases, reduced consumption of such substances on board.

  ➤ **Substitution.** Systematic identification of the dangers of substances can lead to the use of new products which present less of a hazard.

  These may sometimes appear to be weaker than those they replace and people may be sceptical that they will do as good a job. Often, however, they must simply be used in a different way to achieve the same results, while at the same time reducing the risks to health and the environment.

3.5.2 Asbestos

Because of the hazard to long term health which it poses, the use of asbestos on new ships has been banned by most administrations since the end of the 1970s.

There are still a number of older vessels in which asbestos has been used, particularly as gasket or insulation material in the engine room. National administrations' provisions typically stipulate that on existing ships all asbestos that needs repair or renewal, must be replaced by equivalent, but safer, materials.

- **What is asbestos?**

  Asbestos is a generic term for a number of silicate minerals with a finely threaded, flexible structure. It has high heat resistance and is an effective insulator of both heat and electricity.

  All types of asbestos consist of fibres that can easily be separated so that they can be woven into non-flammable materials. Asbestos comes in the form of wool, yarn and board. Typical uses include insulation of pipes, boilers, ovens, heat-resistant gaskets, brake linings and brakepads, in cement products and in protective equipment against high temperatures, such as gloves, aprons, hoods and trousers.

- **The health hazard**

  When individuals inhale asbestos dust, the human body is not capable of breaking down fibres which penetrate the lungs. These cause serious long term illness, including lung cancer. For this reason the sale or use of asbestos has been banned in many countries.

  There are two important dangers which asbestos shares with harmful solvents:

  ➤ The damage it causes is long term. Though the use of protective equipment is mandatory, it is sometimes difficult to persuade younger people to protect themselves against an illness which may not appear for 20–30 years.

  ➤ The combination of working with asbestos and smoking greatly increases the risk of lung cancer. Smoking destroys the cilia in the bronchi, thus reducing the body's ability to stop the thin, sharp asbestos fibres from penetrating the lungs.

- **Identifying the hazard**

  ➤ Identify and record the location and use of any asbestos on board. It is essential for the ship's management to know where asbestos is located and its current condition.

  ➤ All seafarers likely to come in contact with asbestos must be made aware of its location and the dangers it poses.

  ➤ Asbestos that is enclosed will not normally cause emission of dust as long as it is allowed to remain undisturbed.

- **Working with asbestos – not a 'do-it-yourself' activity**

  If asbestos is in poor condition, replacing it with other materials must be considered, particularly if there is any possibility of dust escaping into the ship's atmosphere. Should it be necessary to carry out repairs which include removal of asbestos, this work should be carried out with great care and by specialists.

  In many countries (Norway, for example) firms which remove asbestos must be officially approved to do so. This is an indication of the seriousness of the risk involved.

- **Asbestos – temporary repairs**

  Should it become necessary to carry out temporary repairs to asbestos in poor condition, perhaps because the vessel is at sea:

  ➢ The objective must be to seal the asbestos in. Replacement must be left to specialists.

  ➢ Protective clothing, protective breathing equipment and other safety measures must be used. Expendable boiler suits are recommended.

  ➢ The work area must be carefully screened off and ventilated.

3.6 INFECTIOUS DISEASES and MALARIA

3.6.1 Introduction

Ships are compact work and living environments. In many cases they travel the world, visiting places where seafarers can be exposed to diseases to which they have little resistance. Crews often consist of seafarers of different nationalities and backgrounds, which can increase the potential for and seriousness of cross-infection. All of these factors make ships' environments particularly vulnerable to the spread of infectious diseases.

There are two broad strategies for preventing infection on board:

- **Keep disease off the ship**

  We do this by:

  ➢ Carrying out health checks on new crew members before they join the ship to make sure that they are not about to bring any unwelcome 'visitors' on board and that they have been effectively vaccinated against diseases which they may encounter on the voyage.

  ➢ Rigorous control over the condition of foodstuffs and drinking water brought on board.

- **Prevent disease occurring on the ship**

  High standards of hygiene are an essential defence against the onset of disease on board. Individual seafarers must be encouraged and trained to take responsibility for personal hygiene. The ship's management systems must ensure cleanliness is given high priority. Particular care must be taken in areas and activities associated with food storage, food preparation and waste disposal. The growth of bacteria – tiny living organisms - in water stored on board must be prevented.

3.6.2   Vaccination

The purpose of vaccination is to strengthen the body's defences against particular diseases caused by bacteria and by viruses (these are very small infectious agents that grow in the cells of bacteria, plants and animals, including human beings). The vaccine is a dose of virus or bacteria which has either been weakened or killed so that that it cannot cause disease. Vaccination causes the body to think that it has been exposed to infection. It immediately starts to produce antibodies – protective substances generated when the body detects foreign substances in the bloodstream - against the disease in question.

After vaccination these antibodies are ready to destroy a real infection if it should occur.

3.6.3   Some diseases for which vaccines are available

Note: The information which follows is for general guidance only. **Under no circumstances** must anyone take decisions about their need for vaccination without first consulting a qualified (and, in certain Administrations, accredited) medical practitioner.

Diseases which may be relevant for people working on ships, and for which vaccines exist, include:

- **Diphtheria/tetanus**

  There is a combination vaccine for protection against these two diseases.

  ➢ **Diphtheria** is an acute bacterial infection, where the bacteria produce toxins/poisons that usually attack the tonsils in the throat. The toxin is spread in the blood, where it can attack the heart and nervous system. Diphtheria infects through droplet infection, i.e. small bacteria that are coughed up by an infected person, which then circulate in the air until another person breathes them in and becomes infected. Basic vaccine: 2 doses at a 6-week interval.

  ➢ **Tetanus** is sometimes popularly known as 'lockjaw'. It is an acute bacterial infection that arises in the same way as diphtheria. The bacteria only likes surroundings poor in oxygen, such as wounds. Tetanus infects by the bacteria getting into the body when a wound is polluted, for example by earth, animal saliva, street dirt etc. The toxin affects the muscular nerves and results in stiffness in the musculature. High mortality rate. Basic vaccine: 2 doses at a 6-week interval and a third dose after 1 year.

Revaccination: When someone has received the basic vaccination against diphtheria/tetanus, it is enough to take 1 dose of vaccine at revaccination. Then the vaccine will provide protection for approximately a further 10 years.

- **Poliomyelitis**

This is a viral disease that infects via excrement to the mouth. In connection with large epidemics it also infects via droplets. Norway had a large epidemic in 1951 with 2,200 reported cases. Polio results, amongst other things, in paralysis and muscular dystrophy.

Basic vaccination consists of 3 doses, 2 doses at one month's interval, and the third after 7–12 months. Duration: 5 years.

If more than 10 years have passed since the last polio vaccination, 2 doses of vaccine must be taken at approximately a 4-week interval. If less than 10 years have passed, but more than 5 years since the last dose, one dose, a so-called booster, must be given.

- **Yellow fever**

This extremely serious viral disease is transmitted by mosquito bite. It occurs in Africa, and large parts of South America. The virus attacks the liver and debilitates its function, giving among other things jaundice as one of the symptoms. The disease has a high mortality rate.

The vaccine consists of one dose which provides protection for 10 years. A valid yellow fever vaccination is required for entry into a number of countries.

- **Cholera**

This acute bowel infection with diarrhoea is caused by a bacterium which directly affects the bowels. Infection occurs mainly via polluted water.

There are 2 types of vaccine. An injection provides very poor protection and must be repeated every 6 months. In addition there is an oral vaccine (drinkable vaccine), which provides better protection. The vaccine consists of 2 doses at a 2-6 weeks interval. Duration: 2 years.

- **Hepatitis A/Hepatitis B**

There are separate vaccines against Hepatitis A and Hepatitis B, as well as a combination vaccine for protection against both diseases.

- **Hepatitis A**

This is also a viral disease that attacks the liver. It usually infects via polluted food and drink, but in infrequent cases also sexually.

Since 1992 a vaccine has been developed against hepatitis A. It is found in 2 versions. One consists of 2 doses at an interval of 6–12 months. The other consists of 3 doses, of which the first two are given at approximately a 4-week interval, with a booster dose after 6–12 months. Both provide approximately 10 years' protection after the completed vaccination. Gammaglobulin can also be given against hepatitis A. However, it only provides short-term protection (2-3 months).

- **Hepatitis B**

This is another serious viral disease that attacks the liver and debilitates its function. It infects sexually and via blood and is extremely infectious. After infection some people become chronic carriers of the disease, and may eventually develop cirrhosis of the liver.

The basic vaccination consists of 3 doses. The first two at a 4-week interval, the last one 6 months after the first dose. A blood test is recommended after the final dose to see whether the body has produced sufficient antibodies.

The vaccine provides protection for 5 years after vaccination is completed. The vaccine is strongly recommended for captains/chief officers, or others who are in charge of first aid/treatment of injury.

- **Typhoid fever**

Typhoid is a bowel disease caused by bacteria. It infects via water or polluted foodstuffs.

The vaccine is found in 2 variants: One is taken by injection. The other consists of 3 capsules, one capsule being taken between meals every second day. Both give approximately 3 years' protection.

- **Tuberculosis**

The disease can attack various organs. The most common type attacks the lungs. It infects via coughing and direct contact through sores on the skin, or puncture accidents.

The vaccine is known as the BCG vaccine. Its effectiveness is checked by a test (pirquet or mantoux). Seafarers who are to join Norwegian ships must have been x-rayed and, where necessary, tested.

Contact your local approved seafarer's doctor to have relevant vaccinations updated. If the doctor does not have the vaccine available, he/she can refer you to a vaccination clinic.

3.6.4   Diseases for which no vaccines are available

Two particular diseases which seafarers must be aware of, and for which no vaccine exists, are HIV and Hepatitis C.

- **HIV**

  This virus is transmitted via body fluids, particularly semen and blood. The infection develops into the AIDS disease. There is no vaccine, though certain drugs, often with unpleasant side effects, can slow the onset of full blown AIDS. Mortality is high.

  The most important preventive measures are:

  ➢ Avoid casual sex without protection (condom).

  ➢ Wear gloves when contact may be made with blood or body fluids, for example in connection with the treatment of sores or wounds.

- **Hepatitis C**

  This infects in the same way as HIV. The same protections are strongly recommended.

3.6.5   Malaria

Malarial infection is caused by the bite of a particular mosquito. As a result of the bite a living parasite enters the bloodstream. The disease is still on the increase in many areas around the world. Prevention has gradually become harder as the malaria parasite has developed considerable resistance to the medicines currently in use for prevention and treatment.

In spite of the fact that seafarers are less exposed to infection than others who stay for lengthy periods in a malarial area, preventive medicine must be used. Remember that on board there is no doctor who can make a proper diagnosis and provide adequate treatment immediately.

- **Protection**

  Those who spend time in malarial areas, even only for short periods, must always protect themselves from infection. This is done both by physical protection from being bitten and by taking preventive medicine. For the best protection use both.

  ➢ Protect yourself physically from mosquito bites.

  Try to avoid mosquito bites completely, by covering your body (wear light-coloured, insecticide-treated clothing, long-sleeved shirts and long trousers); by applying topical insect repellent onto exposed skin (35% DEET spray); limit outdoor activities to daytime (the malaria mosquito mainly operates under the cover of darkness – from dusk to dawn); and by sleeping under a mosquito net. Substantial protection results when these approaches are combined, but they may not always work and therefore taking preventative medication in addition is essential.

> ➤ Take preventive medicaments.

Most of the available drugs must be started one week before arrival in the malaria area, continue during the whole stay *and for four weeks after* leaving the malarial area. The reason for continuing to take the medicine so long after departure from the malarial area is that the malarial parasite must be exterminated in the blood stream before the person is safe.

Chloroquine, the former standard drug for malaria prevention and treatment, is now effective only in limited areas. A combination of chloroquinine and proguanil (Paludrine) may be used in areas where parasite resistance to chloroquinine is assessed as moderate. The combination provides better protection than either drug alone, and is both accessible and affordable in those regions where it is commonly recommended, such as the Arabian peninsula, Asia (except for Southeast Asia), Mauritania, Namibia and part of Colombia.

Mefloquine (Lariam) is a highly efficacious drug (>90%) against chloroquine-resistant malaria and has been widely used since the 1980s. Mefloquine is generally well tolerated, side effects are typically mild and self-limited, but occasionally they may be serious (dizziness, headaches, difficulty sleeping, anxiety, depression seizures, delirium). Mefloquine has been provisionally recommended for use over a period up to one year, but pregnant women should avoid using it.

A fixed-dose combination of atovaquone and proguanil (Malarone) was developed in the 1990s for the both the prophylaxis and treatment of multidrug-resistant malaria. Side effects are rare, and it is better tolerated that either mefloquine or chloroquine/proguanil, but should not be used by pregnant women. Because of its short pre- and post-exposure dosing regimens, the drug is ideal for short-term travellers: 1 tablet a day; start 1–2 days before travel and continue for one week after departure from the mainland area.

- **Treatment**

Because the parasite remains active after the person infected leaves the malarial area, it is important that any inexplicable fever that begins after the seventh day of a stay in a malarial area should be considered as possibly caused by malarial infection. Thus, all ships should have medicine that is used for treatment of possible malaria attacks in addition to preventive medication. Radio for advice from a doctor before treating possible malaria attacks

- **The need for protection for those who come from malarial areas**

People from areas where malaria is widespread, and also those who have already been infected by one type of malaria, must also protect themselves, particularly when they are in a different malarial area.

There are four different types of malaria parasite. People who from childhood on have lived in a malarial area eventually develop partial immunity to precisely the type of parasite that is found in that particular area, but not to others. In addition, it is necessary to stay continuously in a particular malarial area to retain partial immunity.

> **NB!**
> *No preventative medication*
> *provides complete protection.*

4. SAFETY AND HEALTH TRAINING

4.0 INTRODUCTION

This section of the manual contains:

1. The principles of safety and health training

- **The legal framework**

  A brief statement of the legal requirements under ISM and an EU Directive.

- **Purpose and Motivation**

  A summary of what shipping companies and individual seafarers regard as the purpose of safety and health training and how that affects seafarers' motivation to take part.

- **Identifying training needs**

  How to involve those who will be on the receiving end of training in the process of deciding what they need.

- **Helping people to learn**

  A summary of how people learn and a simple model describing how to help them do so effectively.

- **Training methods**

  A description of the different tools and approaches available to trainers.

2. How to plan, run, assess and follow up a training session

A summary of the principles of preparation and delivery. What to do after the training is completed.

3. Basic safety training on board

Guidance on the basic content of safety and health training for:

- Shipboard familiarisation

- Safety Supervisors and Safety Officers

- Safety Representatives and the Safety Committee

- Officers and ratings

4.1 PRINCIPLES

4.1.1 The Legal Framework

The ISM Code says that:

The Company should clearly define and document the master's responsibility with regard to:

- *Implementing the safety and environmental policy of the Company*

- *Motivating the crew in the observation of that policy.*

Training has an important role to play in every Master's strategy for meeting these responsibilities.

National and trans-national administrations are often even more specific. The relevant EU Directive, for example, says that:

The employer shall ensure that each worker receives adequate safety and health training, in particular in the form of information and instructions specific to the workstation or job.

And in addition:

The employer shall ensure that workers from outside undertakings and/or establishments engaged in work in his undertaking and/or establishment have in fact received the appropriate instructions regarding health and safety risks.

4.1.2 Purpose and Motivation

Companies and individual seafarers have different perspectives on safety and health training and these naturally affect how they see its purpose.

- **Companies** expect this training to:

  ➤ Help ensure that they meet their legal obligations.

  ➤ Contribute to reducing the costs associated with accidents, injuries and sickness.

- **Individuals** expect this training to:

  ➤ Make them less likely to injure themselves and fall ill.

  ➤ Protect their livelihood and their ability to support themselves and their families.

When designing and delivering training it is important to remember that these different perspectives exist. Individuals are unlikely to be motivated by training which is presented to them as a means of increasing their company's profits! Effective training always focuses on what those being trained regard as attractive outcomes for themselves.

4.1.3 Identifying Training Needs

Much of the work on board ship is relatively routine and covered by standard procedures. There are a number of mandatory subjects for safety training, such as how to carry out abandon ship drills effectively. Risk assessments are also an important way of identifying training needs.

Because of this it is often not difficult for an experienced officer or Safety Supervisor to produce a list of topics to be covered by safety and health training without having to consult anyone else.

Even when that is the case, however, it would be wrong to overlook the advantages of finding out what those who will be trained want and think they need. First of all, doing so helps to focus training more precisely on the details of what is required. For example, all members of fire teams must be able to use breathing equipment properly, but what, specifically, does the particular team you will be training find difficult about doing so? Ask them!

Secondly, it is always more motivating to be asked than to be told. All the evidence tells us that people play a much more active part in training when they have contributed to what it covers and how it is designed.

When finding out about what training people want:

- Ask open questions to encourage them to talk (*'What do you find difficult about …?' 'How would you approach this situation …?'*).

- Avoid asking leading questions (*'Don't you think that …?' 'Wouldn't you agree that …?'*).

- Don't join in! Consultation means asking for people's opinions and listening to them. Try to avoid making statements like *'Well, in my opinion…'*).

- Clarify and summarise. It is often the case that people find it difficult to be precise about the training they think they need. So ask questions to test understanding (*'Have I got this right? Are you saying that …?'*).

- Be patient. When people are unaccustomed to being asked for their opinions it can take time for them to respond. And in some cultures individuals are less inclined to express their opinions in a group than in others.

Experienced trainers often begin training sessions with this type of discussion. It gets the group talking and it helps to focus what will be covered. Most important, it shows the group that the trainer is interested in their views and their experience.

Helping people to learn

Human beings learn in many different ways, but some are more effective than others. In particular:

- **We learn by example**

  This is particularly important in the area of safety. Formal training will give people knowledge and skills, but they will only develop the correct attitude to safe working practices if those around them, especially those senior to them, set a proper example.

- **We learn by explanation**

  Other people tell us what to do or we read what they have written. This works well enough for getting across information and trainers will always have to do a certain amount of 'telling'. But it is not an effective method for imparting skills and it doesn't work at all for changing behaviour. We learn much better when …

- **We learn by demonstration**

  Watching people who know what they are doing demonstrate a skill is a great improvement on listening to them talk about it. But even this method of learning is nothing like as powerful as when …

- **We learn by doing**

  The best way to learn a task is by trying to do it, getting encouragement, guidance and constructive criticism as we do so and then practising until we have mastered it.

Finally:

- **We learn by experience**

  Of course, experience makes some people worse because their unsafe working practices simply get entrenched. Using experience to improve means thinking consciously about what we are doing and how we can learn from it.

  There is a simple model, developed by two British management development specialists, Peter Honey and Alan Mumford, which describes how this process works. It looks like this:

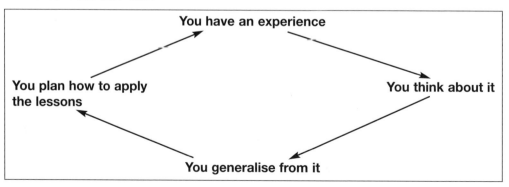

This is a very helpful model when you are planning a training session, because it helps you to put different activities in the right order. For example:

- ➤ **Experience.** The group being trained watch a safety video.

- ➤ **Think about it.** They identify the lessons it contained.

- ➤ **Generalise.** They discuss how to apply these lessons on their ship.

- ➤ **Plan.** They agree specific actions to implement after the training is over.

4.1.5 Training methods

The main methods used for safety training on board ship are:

- **Lectures**

When the trainer has information which the group being trained need to know about, lecturing is the simplest (as well as the cheapest) way of delivering it.

But:

- ➤ **Keep it short.** 10–15 minutes is the maximum amount of time that most people can sit and listen to someone talking at them.

- ➤ **Keep it simple.** Put what you have to say in the everyday language of those you are training. Explain technical terms and acronyms.

- ➤ **Don't read.** Apart from professional actors, very few people can read from a script without sounding dull.

- ➤ **Ask questions.** If what you have to say is going to take longer than ten or fifteen minutes, break the lecture up by asking questions and leading short discussion sessions.

- ➤ **Use examples.** People are often bored by accident statistics and irritated or cynical about rules and regulations. But almost all of us are fascinated by stories of accidents! It is examples that bring the subject of safety to life.

- ➤ **Watch the group** (this is another reason for not reading from a script). Look for signs of puzzlement or boredom. Spot those who want to ask questions.

- **Visuals and props**

A picture, someone said, is worth a thousand words. Use whatever you have got available. Draw on flipcharts. Show overhead transparencies. Use PowerPoint presentations. Give out documents you are going to refer to. Bring along any appropriate equipment – fire extinguishers, safety signs, gas detectors and so on.

- **Training videos**

Training videos are a very powerful way of explaining and dramatising ideas about how people should work together, demonstrating techniques they might use to tackle particular types of situation, providing examples of novel solutions to common problems and showing situations, such as serious fires, which for obvious reasons cannot be duplicated on board.

They work particularly well if they are used as an integrated part of the session. Don't simply use them as a filler. Remember that you don't have to use the whole video or play it without interruption. You can:

➢ Rewind it to show a particularly important section again.

➢ Stop for discussion. Some videos will show you the wrong way to do something, followed by the right way. Stop the tape and find out what the group think is being done incorrectly and then use the illustration of the right way to confirm the ideas they have come up with.

- **Discussion**

It is essential to encourage those being trained to identify and commit themselves to actions they will take to make their lives on board safer. Discussion of how the information, techniques and ideas covered in the training relate to their circumstances should be a major part of any safety training session. When leading a discussion:

➢ Ask open questions.

➢ Give people time to answer. Sometimes you simply have to wait. Silence is an effective way of prompting someone to answer. Once one person speaks, others normally follow.

➢ Use small groups. If people seem reluctant to speak out in larger groups, break them into small groups and ask each small group to appoint a spokesperson.

- **Distance and 'e' learning**

Not all training has to be in groups. Individual study can also be a useful means of acquiring information (though not, obviously, of strengthening group safety culture). The methods used can be as simple as reading a book or they can involve the use of a computer and the growing volume of 'e-learning' software.

CDs and, increasingly, DVDs are important tools for self-study. Properly designed, they can make what is inevitably a rather solitary activity interesting and interactive.

Effective learning from computer based training requires:

➤ **Clear objectives.** This is true of all training, but it is even more important when working without the help of a human trainer. There is more about setting objectives for training under 'How to prepare' below.

➤ **'Little and often'.** Active people like seafarers can find it particularly hard to concentrate for any length of time when sitting passively in front of a computer. Use software which breaks subjects down into modules.

➤ **Variety.** Well designed e-learning material minimises the disadvantage of the learner working alone by using video clips, graphics and so on to make the experience as interesting as possible.

➤ **Interaction.** Look for programmes which make learners work. Well designed programmes have built in questions to test their understanding and workbook functions which ask them to relate what they are learning to the circumstances on their ships.

For the best results computer based training must be integrated with discussion and application. The best designed programmes will contain guidance on how to do so.

4.2   HOW TO PLAN, RUN, ASSESS AND FOLLOW UP A TRAINING SESSION

4.2.1   Preparation

Spending time on preparation buys you peace of mind. Think about:

• **What you know (and don't know) about the subject**

There is nothing quite like teaching other people about a subject to focus your mind on what you do and don't know about it. You must, at all costs, avoid the horrible realisation in the middle of a training session that you are only one page ahead of the group. So, during preparation, identify any gaps in your knowledge and plan how to fill them.

• **The group you will be training**

➤ **Size.** Six to ten is normally the ideal sized group for one person to handle. It is difficult to control a group larger than ten so that everyone is able to contribute.

Though a group of less than six allows you to give a lot of attention to individuals, there is the potential disadvantage that either one or two strong personalities can swamp the rest or that you end up with three or four quiet people, none of whom will say a word. Which leads to the second point ...

➤ **Individuals.** Think about whether individual members of the group have any particular experience on which you can draw during the session. Think about personalities – who are the quiet ones? The extroverts? The cynics? How will you deal with them?

- **Your objectives**

  You must be absolutely clear what you want to achieve. Everything else flows from that. Objectives come from:

  ➤ the subject you want to cover

  ➤ the group's existing knowledge and skills

  ➤ the time you have available.

  It is better to achieve a modest training objective than miss an ambitious one. If the topic is large, break the objective down into manageable stages and tackle it over a number of sessions.

  Objectives for a training session should tell you what those taking part will be able to do as a result. For example:

  > *As a result of this training those taking part will be able to operate the type of breathing equipment carried on this ship*

  Write your objectives down and keep them beside you when you are preparing the structure of the session. This will help you to avoid going down interesting, but irrelevant, side tracks.

- **How to structure the session**

  Objectives tell you where you want to end up. The next stages in structuring the session are:

  ➤ **Building blocks.** Write down all the major areas you will have to cover to achieve the objectives. Don't worry about detail or sequence at this point.

  ➤ **Sequence.** Put the building blocks in logical order.

  ➤ **Time check.** Do a rough time check, before you put in a lot of detailed work. You know how long you have available for the whole session. Now that you have the outline structure in front of you, ask yourself whether you can realistically cover all of it, given the need to involve the group and avoid delivering a lecture at breakneck pace. If the answer is no, go back to the objectives and scale them down.

  ➤ **Plan each building block in turn.** Use an appropriate mixture of lectures, demonstrations, group involvement, visual aids and so on. Variety adds interest.

  ➤ **Another time check.** Once you have planned the details of each building block, you can then do a more exact estimate of the total time needed and make any adjustments necessary.

106

➢ **Notes.** By this stage you will have a detailed plan of what you are going to cover and how you are going to do so. The next step is to prepare notes from which to run the session.

Many people find that A4 sheets in a ring binder are the best way to organise these so that they are in the right order and don't get muddled up while you are training.

Remember that notes are supposed to be memory joggers, not a text from which to read, so don't put in too much detail. Make sure that you have a note of facts, such as statistics of particular types of accidents, which you want to quote and must get right.

➢ **Anticipate questions.** It is always easier to think of answers to questions during preparation than when you are on your feet in front of the group. So spend some time thinking about what you might be asked.

➢ **Written summaries.** Decide whether you want the group to take away any written summaries of what you have covered. If you do, make sure you keep these short and simple.

• **The setting**

One great advantage which running safety training on board has over shore based training establishments is access to the most important piece of training equipment of all – the ship. This means, for example, that you do not have to show people pictures of watertight doors. You can show them the real ones.

When you are delivering training in a training room, think about how you want people to sit, because that will affect how you all communicate with one another.

Different room layouts suit different purposes.

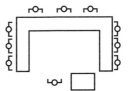

Theatre style	**An open square**	**Round a table**
Use this layout for briefing sessions, when you want to give the group information and answer questions without starting a debate.	With this layout the trainer is the central figure, but it is easy to start a discussion amongst the group since they can all make eye contact with one another.	This layout encourages discussion without over-emphasising the role of the group leader. A round table is better than a rectangular one for this purpose.

Delivering a training session

- **Don't worry!**

  ➤ Nerves are natural.

  ➤ You control them with preparation and practice.

  ➤ However you feel, *look* confident (open body posture, eye contact).

  ➤ *Remember*, people only see what you look like, they can't tell how you feel.

- **Don't rush - you're in charge**

  ➤ Make sure you are ready.

  ➤ Wait till you have their attention.

  ➤ Make eye contact.

  ➤ Look friendly – smile!

  ➤ Politely interrupt any whispered conversations going on.

- **No magical mystery tours!**

  First you tell them what you're going to tell them. Then you tell them. Then you tell them what you've told them

  In other words, at the beginning of a training session explain:

  ➤ The objectives - what they will know or be able to do as a result of the training.

  ➤ The outline programme.

  ➤ How the session will be run.

  ➤ What you expect from them (for example, whether you want questions during or after the session).

- **Ask for a reaction**

  For example:

  ➤ Are there any questions?

  ➤ What do they want from the session?

- **Get them going**

  Unless the session is going to be very short, try to get the group talking or doing something as early in the session as you can.

Good training delivery depends on The 2Ss, Structure and Style

- **Structure**

  There are three stages:

  - ➤ **Setting the scene.** In your introduction, put the topic in context, describe what those taking part will be able to do when the training is complete, and explain how you are going to run the session.

    It is very important to stress that you want the group to contribute, by asking questions, discussing and, if appropriate, practising any tasks you are going to explain and demonstrate.

  - ➤ **Bit by bit.** Take the topic stage by stage, using the appropriate mixture of training methods you have prepared.

  - ➤ **Summarising.** Remember *'First you tell them …'!* At the end of each stage and at the end of the session, summarise.

- **Style**

  Good trainers have a style which is:

  - ➤ **Clear.** This is where preparation counts. If you have broken the topic down into logical stages you will never find yourself having to confuse the group by saying something like *'hang on a minute, I should have told you earlier about …'.*

    In addition, be careful to explain the meaning of technical terms and acronyms.

  - ➤ **Positive.** Enthusiasm is infectious. Show those being trained that you think the topic is important, to them as well as the company.

  - ➤ **Participative.** Give them practise. Encourage discussion. The best way to do this is to be …

  - ➤ **Inquisitive.** Try to ask questions as much as you can, so that individuals have to think as well as listen.

  - ➤ **Observant.** You can almost always tell more about people's interest and understanding by watching them than by listening to what they say. Watch out for people who say *'yes I understand'* when their body language is telling you that they don't.

4.2.3   **Assessment and follow up**

Once a training session is over it is important to find out whether it has been effective and what, if anything, needs to be altered or improved the next time the session is run. That involves looking for answers to three questions:

1 How satisfied with the training are those who took part?

2 What suggestions do they have for modifications or improvements

3 To what extent are they applying what they have learned?

- **Measuring satisfaction**

  The simplest way to do this is to use a questionnaire. A typical example is shown below. When designing your own version, think about:

  ➢ Whether to use open or closed questions or a mixture. A compromise is to use a rating scale.

  ➢ Whether the questionnaire should be anonymous.

Training Evaluation Form

4 To what extent did the course meet your expectations?

❏ 75-100%   ❏ 50-75%   ❏ 25-50%   ❏ less than 25%

What were the most interesting topics covered?

What were the least interesting topics covered?

On a scale of 1 – 10, rate the extent to which you will be able to apply what you have learned in your daily work (1 = not at all 10 = fully).

On a scale of 1 – 5, rate effectiveness of the following teaching methods used (1 = not effective 5 = fully effective)

❏ Lecturing   ❏ Group work   ❏ Group discussions

❏ Practical work with colleagues   ❏ Individual discussion with instructor

❏ Practical demonstration or info at the working place

❏ Computer assisted aids   ❏ Video

Was the pace ...

❏ Too fast?   ❏ Too slow?   ❏ About right?

Was the documentation ...

❏ Very useful?   ❏ Useful?   ❏ Not useful?

On a scale of 1 – 10, how do you rate the standard of presentation?
1 = poor 10 = excellent

Any other comments

- **Identifying improvements**

  When you have run a training session there are two sources of ideas for improvement – yourself and those who took part.

  ➢ Use the learning model outlined earlier to de-brief yourself. What went well? What went less well? Did the timings work? How effective were the various visuals and props? And so on. Use your conclusions to plan improvements.

  ➢ Add an open ended 'suggestions' question to the questionnaire.

- **Monitoring application**

  After an appropriate period, follow up the training by talking both to those who took part and to their officers. Find out:

  ➢ What people remember about the training.

  ➢ What they are finding useful.

  ➢ What they are doing differently as a result.

4.3   **BASIC SAFETY TRAINING ON BOARD**

There are some basic topics which you should cover whatever your type of ship and trading pattern. Some of these are mandatory, legal requirements. Add to them to suit your ship's specific circumstances.

4.3.1   **Shipboard familiarisation**

The Seafarers' Training, Certification and Watchkeeping (STCW) Code (Chapter VI, Section A-VI/1), stipulates that:

'Before being assigned to shipboard duties, all persons employed or engaged on a seagoing ship, other than passengers, must receive approved familiarisation training in personal survival techniques, or receive sufficient information and instruction, taking account of the guidance given in part B, to be able to …'

Note that:

- The Code says that they must be trained *'Before being assigned to shipboard duties'.*

- The Code says *'to be able to'.* This is not simply about giving people information. They must be able to perform the activities specified.

The specified activities are:

1.1 communicate with other persons on board on elementary safety matters and understand safety information symbols, signs and alarm signals

1.2 know what to do if:

    1.2.1 a person falls overboard

    1.2.2 fire or smoke is detected, or

    1.2.3 the fire or abandon ship alarm is sounded

1.3 identify muster and embarkation stations and emergency escape routes

1.4 locate and don lifejackets

1.5 raise the alarm and have basic knowledge of the use of portable fire extinguishers

1.6 take immediate action upon encountering an accident or other medical emergency before seeking further medical assistance on board; and

1.7 close and open the fire, weathertight and watertight doors fitted in the particular ship other than those for hull openings

---

Further safety training is required for those with specific safety or pollution control duties.

The ISM Code says that:

'The Company should establish procedures to ensure that new personnel and personnel transferred to new assignments related to safety and protection of the environment are given proper familiarisation with their duties. Instructions which are essential to be provided prior to sailing should be identified, documented and given'

The Chapter and Section of STCW quoted above goes on to cover the requirements for individuals with these duties in some detail. The basic regulation is set out below. Refer to your copy of the STCW Code for the details contained in the tables listed.

2   Seafarers employed or engaged in any capacity on board ship on the business of that ship as part of the ship's complement with designated safety or pollution-prevention duties in the operation of the ship shall, before being assigned to any shipboard duties:

    2.1   receive appropriate approved basic training or instruction in:

        2.1.1 personal survival techniques as set out in table A-VI/1-1,

        2.1.2 fire prevention and fire fighting as set out in table A-VI/1-2,

        2.1.3 elementary first aid as set out in table A-VI/1-3, and

        2.1.4 personal safety and social responsibilities as set out in table A-VI/1-4.

    2.2   be required to provide evidence of having achieved the required standard of competence to undertake the tasks, duties and responsibilities listed in column 1 of tables A-VI/1-1, A-VI/1-2, A-VI/1-3 and A-VI/1-4 within the previous five years through:

        2.2.1 demonstration of competence, in accordance with the methods and the criteria for evaluating competence tabulated in columns 3 and 4 of those tables; and

        2.2.2 examination or continuous assessment as part of an approved training programme in the subjects listed in column 2 of those tables.

The STCW Code gives Administrations the option to exempt ships, other than passenger ships of more than 500 grt engaged on international voyages and tankers, from the full requirements of this section if it considers these to be unreasonable or impractical.

Check whether this exemption applies to your ship.

4.3.2   Safety Supervisors and Safety Officers

Here is a list of subjects which those with particular responsibility for safety and health on board must understand. Many of these also require the ability to put procedures into practice and implement improvements.

- The ISM Code
- The role of the Safety Officer/Supervisor
- The Safety Committee
- Risk Assessment
- Safety Inspections
- Accident investigations
- Permits to Work
- Shipboard Familiarisation
- Safety Training
- Drills
- Promoting a safety culture on board

4.3.3 **Safety Representatives and the Safety Committee**

It is not essential for Safety Representatives and other members of the Safety Committee to have quite the same depth of understanding as the Safety Supervisor of, for example, how to carry out risk assessments and safety inspections, but they should have a thorough grasp of the principles.

- Preparing for and taking part in meetings

- Risk assessment

- Safety inspections

- Accident investigations

- Safety regulations relevant to the ship

4.3.4 **Officers and Ratings**

The STCW Code describes in great detail the standard of competence required by ships officers and ratings. The Code defines 'standard of competence' as:

'the level of proficiency to be achieved for the proper performance of functions on board ship in accordance with the internationally agreed criteria as set forth herein (i.e. in the Code) and incorporating prescribed standards or levels of knowledge, understanding and demonstrated skill'

When planning safety training, use the STCW standards as your guide.

5. REVIEWING SAFETY AND HEALTH ON BOARD

5.0 INTRODUCTION

The purpose of this Section of the manual is to help the Safety Supervisor and the Safety Committee to review the crew's perceptions about safety on board and, in particular, areas where they believe that standards could be improved.

The Section contains:

- **A questionnaire for finding out what the crew thinks**

  This covers their perceptions of:

  ➤ Safety information

  ➤ Safety documentation

  ➤ Safety equipment and ergonomics

  ➤ Assessment of risks

  ➤ Health on board

  ➤ Safety and health training

  ➤ Permits to Work

  ➤ Crew participation in safety on board

  ➤ Company involvement in safety on board

  ➤ Crew members' attitudes to risk

  Most of the questions first ask the crew member to tick 'yes', 'no' or 'not sure' about specific details of the topic and then to give an overall 'score' of effectiveness between 1 (poor/ineffective etc.) and 5 (excellent etc.).

- **A form on which to summarise the crew's opinions**

  This simple form allows you to display the average response to the 'overall effectiveness' part of each question. You can, of course, provide the crew with a much more detailed summary by giving them the total number of 'yes', 'no' and 'not sure' answers for each question.

  We recommend using this questionnaire regularly, say every 3 to 6 months. This will provide you with an assessment of the effectiveness of actions you have taken to improve safety.

  (Note that this procedure is not required as part of annual reporting of safety to national administrations.)

  (Note: You may photocopy the questionnaire and summary form for use on board your ship.)

5.1   **ORGANISATION OF SAFETY AND HEALTH ON BOARD**

A questionnaire for individual members of the crew

5.1.1   **Introduction**

The purpose of this questionnaire is to help the Safety Supervisor and the Safety Committee find out what the crew think about the strengths and weaknesses of safety and health management on board. This will enable them to decide on the priorities of actions to make this ship a safer and healthier place for all of us to work and live.

Most of the questions first ask you to tick 'yes', 'no' or 'not sure' about specific details of the topic and then to give an overall 'score' of effectiveness between 1 (poor/ineffective etc.) and 5 (excellent etc.).

You do not have to put your name on the Questionnaire. The information you provide is completely confidential.

Once the Committee has put together all of the views from you and your fellow seafarers they will publish a summary.

5.1.2   **Questionnaire**

Q1: Information about safety and health

How do you rate the information about safety and health which you are provided with on board?

1	2	3	4	5
Poor		Average		Excellent

Q2: Documentation on safety and health

Written procedures, permits, safety notices and so on form an important part of your ship's safety system. How do you rate the quality of this documentation on safety and health?

	Yes	No
• Documents are easy to find	❑	❑
• They cover all relevant issues	❑	❑
• They are easy to understand	❑	❑
• They are regularly updated	❑	❑

How do you rate the overall quality of the safety and health documentation on board?

1	2	3	4	5
Poor		Average		Excellent

Q3: Safety equipment and ergonomics

Ships carry a range of equipment, from mechanical handling devices to ear protectors, to help you carry out your work safely. How do you rate this equipment? How well is both the equipment and the organisation of work adapted to suit the characteristics of individuals?

	Yes	No	Not sure
• There is suitable safety equipment for everyone on board.	❑	❑	❑
• Due consideration is given to differences in skill/body size/strength.	❑	❑	❑
• Individual differences are allowed for:			
➤ Firefighters' suits come in different sizes	❑	❑	❑
➤ Survival suits fit the individuals who use them	❑	❑	❑
• Safety railings are provided where necessary.	❑	❑	❑
• Sharp edges at head height are protected.	❑	❑	❑
• There are warning signs for hazardous spaces.	❑	❑	❑
• Safety harness/lifelines are always available.	❑	❑	❑
• Appropriate protective equipment is always issued before work is started.	❑	❑	❑
• Damaged protective equipment is repaired or discarded.	❑	❑	❑
• Breathing apparatus is regularly and properly inspected and maintained.	❑	❑	❑
• Care is taken to ensure that no member of a search and rescue team suffers from claustrophobia.	❑	❑	❑
• Care is taken to ensure that no-one suffering from vertigo (a fear of heights) is required to work aloft.	❑	❑	❑

Overall, how do you rate the equipment provided on board to enable you to do your job safely?

1	2	3	4	5
Poor		Average		Excellent

Overall, how well are the equipment and the organisation of work adapted to suit the characteristics of individuals?

1	2	3	4	5
Not at all		Reasonably		Very well

Q4: Assessment of risks

	Yes	No	Not sure
• Is there a formal procedure for assessing risks on board?	❏	❏	❏

If you are aware of a formal system for assessing risks on board, how well do you think it works?

1	2	3	4	5
Badly		Average		Very Well

Q5: Health on board

	Yes	No	Not sure
• Did you have a medical examination before joining this ship?	❏	❏	❏
• Were you made aware of any particular health precautions for working on this ship, such as recommended vaccinations?	❏	❏	❏
• Were the results of any medical examinations and/or vaccination certificates checked when you joined the ship?	❏	❏	❏
• Are you satisfied with the facilities for treating injuries on this ship?	❏	❏	❏

How stressful is working on this ship?

1	2	3	4	5
Very stressful		Reasonably stressful		Not stressful

How do you rate the standard of cleanliness and hygiene on this ship?

1	2	3	4	5
Poor		Reasonable		Excellent

How do you rate the precautions taken for handling dangerous materials, such as chemicals and solvents, on this ship?

1	2	3	4	5
Poor		Reasonable		Excellent

Q6: Safety and health training

	Yes	No
• Did you receive any safety and health training before joining this ship?	❏	❏
• Did you receive basic safety familiarisation training after signing on, but before taking up your duties?	❏	❏
• Since joining the ship have you received training in the following subjects?	❏	❏
➢ Manual handling?	❏	❏
➢ Protection against noise and vibration?	❏	❏
➢ Use of personal protective equipment?	❏	❏
➢ The Company's Permit to Work system?	❏	❏
➢ Dealing with emergencies (fire; abandon ship etc)	❏	❏
➢ Dangerous materials: safety and health risks and precautions?	❏	❏

How do you rate the standard of safety and health training on board?

1	2	3	4	5
Poor		Reasonable		Excellent

Q7: Permits to Work

Are you aware of any work being done without the issuing of a formal Permit to Work:

	Yes	No
• In tanks or other enclosed spaces?	❏	❏
• Aloft?	❏	❏

How satisfied are you with the operation of the Permit to Work system on this ship?

1	2	3	4	5

Not at all satisfied	Fairly satisfied	Very satisfied

Q8: Crew participation in safety onboard

	Yes	No	Not sure
• All categories of crew member are actively involved	❏	❏	❏
• Safety work is relevant for ratings only	❏	❏	❏
• Everybody is free to ask questions or make suggestions about safety	❏	❏	❏
• The Safety Committee has the required number of meetings	❏	❏	❏

How do you rate the effectiveness of the Safety Committee?

1	2	3	4	5

Not effective	Reasonably effective	Very effective

How active is the crew in maintaining and improving safety onboard?

1	2	3	4	5

Not active	Reasonably active	Very active

Q9: The support provided by the Company to safety and health onboard

	Yes	No	Not sure
• The Company is actively involved in supporting safety and health onboard	❑	❑	❑
• The Company has qualified people supporting us	❑	❑	❑
• The Company pays attention to our safety reports	❑	❑	❑
• The Company actively follows up accident reports to identify the causes	❑	❑	❑
• The Company provides us with useful information to help us improve safety on board	❑	❑	❑

What is your overall opinion of the support which the Company provides to maintain and improve safety and health onboard?

1	2	3	4	5
Poor		Average		Excellent

Q10: Your personal attitude to work involving risk

This question is about the state of the safety culture on board and, in particular, the extent to which all members of the crew think actively about safety as they go about their work. Please try to be as honest with yourself as possible when answering this question. Remember that your answers will remain entirely confidential.

You will find that your answers will be more accurate if you think about them in the context of specific examples of work involving potential risks which you have carried out on board.

	Always	Sometimes	Never
• When you see someone doing something risky or dangerous, do you warn them?	❑	❑	❑
• When you are working on potentially hazardous jobs, do you …			
➢ expect to receive information about the risks involved?	❑	❑	❑
➢ discuss the risks with the Safety Supervisor?	❑	❑	❑
➢ check that safeguards are in place before starting work?	❑	❑	❑
➢ make sure that you are using the correct personal protective equipment?	❑	❑	❑
➢ discuss the risks with everyone involved?	❑	❑	❑
➢ make sure that everyone involved understands and is using the correct safety precautions?	❑	❑	❑

How do you rate your overall attitude to safety?

1	2	3	4	5
I take too many chances		I am reasonably careful		I put safety first every time

A SUMMARY OF RESPONSES TO THE SAFETY AND HEALTH QUESTIONNAIRE

This summary shows the average response to the 'overall effectiveness' part of each of the 9 questions on the questionnaire.

Total number of questionnaires distributed	
Number of questionnaires returned	
Percentage response	

Question	Average response: 1 = poor (or equivalent); 5 = excellent (or equivalent)
Safety information How do you rate the information about safety and health which you are provided with on board?	
Safety documentation How do you rate the overall quality of the safety and health documentation on board?	
Safety equipment and ergonomics Overall, how do you rate the equipment provided on board to enable you to do your job safely?	
Overall, how well is the equipment and the organisation of work adapted to suit the characteristics of individuals?	
Risk Assessment If you are aware of a formal system for assessing risks on board, how well do you think it works?	
Health How stressful is working on this ship? How do you rate the standard of cleanliness and hygiene on this ship?	
How do you rate the precautions taken for handling dangerous materials, such as chemicals and solvents, on this ship?	
Permits to Work How satisfied are you with the operation of the Permit to Work system on this ship?	
Crew participation in safety on board How do you rate the effectiveness of the Safety Committee?	
How active is the crew in maintaining and improving safety onboard?	
Company support for safety and health on board What is your overall opinion of the support which the Company provides to maintain and improve safety and health onboard?	
Crew members' attitude to safety How do you rate your overall attitude to safety?	

6. THE HUMAN FACTOR

6.0 SAFETY CULTURE

The application of the ISM Code should support and encourage the development of a Safety Culture in shipping [IMO Resolution A.788 (19), Guidelines on the Implementation of the International Safety Management (ISM) Code]

The steps taken by shipping companies to put the ISM Code into practice inevitably, and correctly, result in safety management becoming more formal and systematic. Policies are defined, procedures are written, records are kept. That is all as it should be, but it is not enough. On its own, paperwork will not prevent a single injury. Dramatic improvements in safety only come about when individuals think about and take responsibility for their own safety and that of their fellow seafarers. There must be a culture on board every ship in which safety comes first.

6.0.1 What is 'safety culture'?

The figure below shows the main elements of a safety culture.

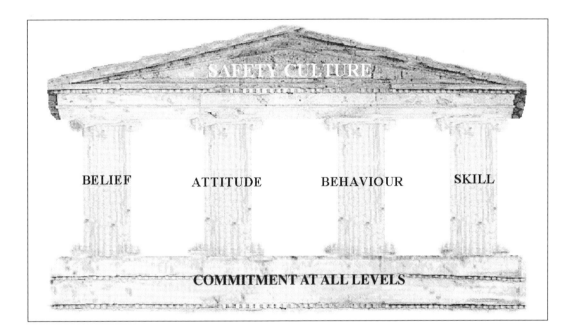

* **The foundation**

   We need look no further than the ISM Code for a definition of the foundation on which an effective safety culture rests:

   The cornerstone of good safety management is commitment from the top. In matters of safety and pollution prevention it is the commitment, competence, attitudes and motivation of individuals at all levels that determines the end result. [ISM Code, Preamble, para. 6]

Companies demonstrate commitment to safety in the following ways:

> **Structure**

The ISM Code requires companies to describe the functions of all those responsible for safety and also to designate the person or persons ashore who will provide the link between the company and those on board.

The Code says that the designated person must have direct access to the highest level of management. To effectively demonstrate commitment to safety it is essential that this access is seen to be in operation by everyone on board.

> **Policy**

Safe working practices must be set out and supported by clear statements of policy.

> **Communication**

Managers ashore, superintendents and others visiting ships, together with officers on board, must continuously communicate the importance of safety. The goal must be to become almost boringly obsessive about the subject.

> **Action**

Action is the most important evidence of management commitment. Unfortunately there are organisations which practice the opposite of what they preach. They are just paying lip service to the subject and their employees recognise this and act accordingly.

For example, though a company may have a legally acceptable, written environmental protection policy, if all that the crew hear about from their managers ashore is a continual stress on the high cost of legal discharge of sludge, garbage and sewage in port and the need to save money, no-one should be surprised if they resort to illegal discharge at sea.

• **Belief**

Individual seafarers must believe that safety is important. It may seem obvious that they should do so since no-one, surely, wants to get hurt. But it is not quite as simple as that. Because the nature of seafarers' work is more physically demanding and inherently hazardous than, say, working in an office, there can be a tendency to regard a concern for safety as somehow 'weak'. One of the authors of this manual came across an example of this state of mind when he was told, when working in a shipyard as a young man, that *'you can't be a proper engineer if you've got ten fingers!'*

It is not possible to create a strong safety culture if people believe that safety is for softies.

- **Attitude**

Creating a safety culture often involves changing the way people think. What attitude do some people have to safety? Here are some examples:

'It won't happen to me'

'The officers and the Safety Supervisor look after safety. It's their job, not mine'

'There's a procedure for this, so I don't need to worry'

'It's not my business to point out other people's unsafe actions'

'Safety precautions are all very well for inexperienced youngsters. But I've been at sea for twenty years. I know what corners I can cut'

- **Behaviour**

It is particularly important for the senior and more experienced individuals on board to behave in ways which demonstrate that, for them, safety comes first. Example is the most effective way of creating a strong safety culture.

- **Skill**

As Dr Heinrich pointed out, skilled and experienced people working in unsafe situations can have a better safety record than unqualified and inexperienced people working in safe situations. While it must be the goal of everyone on board to make working conditions as safe as possible, unless those involved are competent, accidents will happen however many precautions are taken.

6.0.2 Practical questions for Managers and Officers

There are a number of actions which managers and officers can take to strengthen the safety culture on board. The answers to the following questions will help to identify what is appropriate in the particular circumstances of each ship.

- **What management does**

  - Does management actively and visibly support safety? (what examples are there to justify answering 'yes' to this question?)

  - Are sufficient resources always available for safety (even if providing them means adjusting the allocated budget)?

  - Is safety an issue which is always discussed at management meetings?

- **What management pays attention to**

  - Does management pay attention to the crews' injury and illness records and trends?

> Do managers systematically investigate the safety implications of change - new ships, new equipment, modified processes, different cargoes, changes to chemicals or materials and so on?

- **What management ignores**

  > Does management pay insufficient attention to shipboard workplace hazards, poorly designed working practices, operations, materials handling and transportation?

- **What measures and controls management uses**

  > Is the control and inspection of safety adequate?

  > Do operational matters ever come before employees' safety?

  > Are injuries and illnesses under-reported?

  > Is the reporting of near misses encouraged (and does it happen)?

  > Is the mandatory reporting of personal injuries to the relevant Administration communicated to the appropriate managers?

  There is an obvious danger in regarding 'management' as a group of people who are in constant and perfect communication with one another. Very few organisations with more than one manager succeed in achieving this happy state of affairs! It is very important that the department responsible for informing the Administration about accidents and injuries also passes this information to those colleagues within the company who are in a position to draw lessons from what has happened and take steps to prevent similar situations from arising in the future.

- **How management responds to accidents and unsafe acts**

  > Are accidents systematically investigated?

  > Are near misses systematically investigated?

  > What is the primary purpose of accident and unsafe act investigations – to determine the cause or to apportion blame?

  > Do investigations cover any possible managerial responsibility?

6.1   UNDERSTANDING ACCIDENTS

6.1.1   Introduction

The struggle to improve safety at work is, of course, not unique to shipping and there is an enormous amount which our industry can learn from the work which has been carried out over a very long period in other industries.

Perhaps the most important lessons are, first, the importance of the human factor in improving safety and, second, the fact that the often expressed dilemma of having to choose between efficiency and cost on the one hand and safety on the other is false. As the great quality expert Dr W E Deming put it:

*Since the beginning of the industrial revolution, a constant conflict has existed between production efficiency and safety. A new approach that blends safety attitudes and behaviour patterns within production is needed. Because priorities always change, this approach must stress safety as a **human value** rather than priorities. The need for safety is a **human right**, which cannot be outranked by operational priorities. This new approach must stress the Human Factor in operation, which again is highly influenced by the employee's attitudes and behaviour. How well people are educated, trained and treated is more important than the actual work process.*

6.1.2 The Safety Iceberg

Earlier in the manual we referred to the relationship between serious accidents and near misses. This accident distribution model is one of the principal findings from Dr H W Heinrich's ground breaking work on safety 'Industrial Accident Prevention' which he published in 1931. The model is often described (in words which are particularly appropriate for seafarers) as a Safety Iceberg.

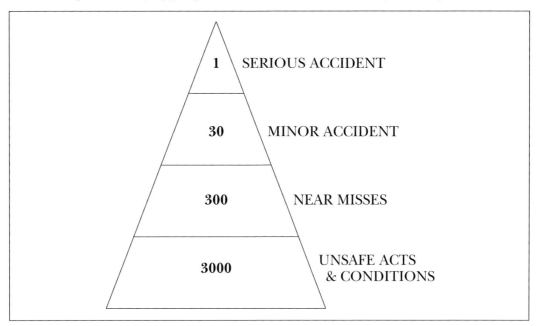

6.1.3 Accidents – the basic causes

Though the proportions of the iceberg which make up the different layers vary depending on the type of operation, it is generally accepted that there is a relationship between the various outcomes. Cut down on unsafe acts and conditions, investigate and follow up near misses and the number of more serious accidents will decline.

So, if we are going to pay close attention, not merely to the occasional serious accident, but to the very much larger number of near misses, unsafe acts and conditions, it is helpful to be aware of how the human factor causes accidents to arise.

There are two basic causes of accidents:

- Unsafe acts by individuals

- Unsafe working conditions

Dr Heinrich expands on these in the following Accident Causation Model.

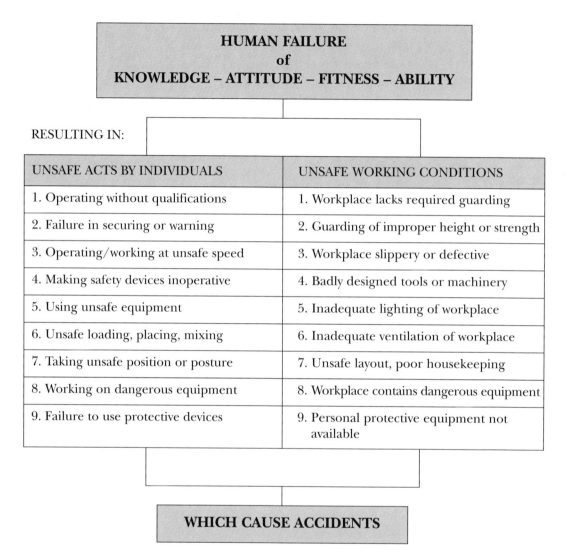

HUMAN FAILURE of KNOWLEDGE – ATTITUDE – FITNESS – ABILITY	

RESULTING IN:

UNSAFE ACTS BY INDIVIDUALS	UNSAFE WORKING CONDITIONS
1. Operating without qualifications	1. Workplace lacks required guarding
2. Failure in securing or warning	2. Guarding of improper height or strength
3. Operating/working at unsafe speed	3. Workplace slippery or defective
4. Making safety devices inoperative	4. Badly designed tools or machinery
5. Using unsafe equipment	5. Inadequate lighting of workplace
6. Unsafe loading, placing, mixing	6. Inadequate ventilation of workplace
7. Taking unsafe position or posture	7. Unsafe layout, poor housekeeping
8. Working on dangerous equipment	8. Workplace contains dangerous equipment
9. Failure to use protective devices	9. Personal protective equipment not available

WHICH CAUSE ACCIDENTS

There are two important points to recognise about the model:

- First, unsafe working conditions are also a consequence of human failure, often on the part of management. Accidents cannot be excused because '*the system failed*' or '*the procedure couldn't cope in these circumstances*'. Systems and procedures do not have a life of their own. They are designed and implemented by human beings.

- Second, there is a close and not always simple connection between systems and equipment and those who are expected to operate them. To quote from the USCG 'Guide to the application of human factors engineering':

  '*The human is the most complex component in the ship/system interface. Designing equipment or software to be used on a ship without considering the humans who will use and maintain them will lead to less than an optimum match between the human and the machine.*'

Human behaviour

Using unsafe equipment or allowing dangerous equipment into a workplace is, on the face of it, seriously irrational behaviour. So why do people do it? There are two sets of factors:

• Basic motivation

• Personal ability and attitude

By understanding and working on both of these we can prevent many accidents from taking place.

• **Basic motivation**

When an officer sees a rating doing something unsafe it is not uncommon for him to say '*Wake up!*'. Sometimes people are so disinterested in their work that can appear to be almost asleep.

It is not possible to generate the correct level of enthusiasm and concern for safety amongst people whose work fails to motivate them. Social scientists who study the relationship between motivation and performance at work are generally agreed that the following factors determine whether people are likely to feel motivated.

➤ **Satisfactory and meaningful job content**

Work, even unpleasant work, becomes much more acceptable when we understand why we are doing it, when we can see that we have achieved a satisfactory result and when we believe that result to be worthwhile.

➤ **Variety**

An unrelieved diet of chipping paint or cleaning bilges will soon dampen the enthusiasm of the most dedicated seafarer.

➤ **Challenge and development**

Brains are human beings most important attribute. It motivates us to be given the opportunity to use them.

➤ **Responsibility and control**

Human beings are not robots. It is an almost universal finding that performance and safety improve, often dramatically, when people are given responsibility for and an appropriate measure of control over their work.

➤ **Support and recognition**

In organisations whose employees are highly motivated, managers see their primary role as being to remove whatever constraints are preventing their staff from doing a better job and to provide them with praise and encouragement when they do good work.

> ### Socially acceptable work

Work becomes more motivating when we can see that it contributes to a wider purpose which is valued by other people.

> ### Career progression

Though many of us reach a stage in our lives when we are content with the job we have (assuming it meets the criteria above), career progression, particularly when we are younger, can be an important motivator.

- ## Personal ability and attitude

Though accidents can result from many different types of human error, safety professionals recognise that some are much more common than others, particularly the six types described below. For safety's sake it is essential to take these into account when making decisions about equipment and its uses or operating procedures.

> ### Lack of skill, knowledge, aptitude or physical ability

Many accidents are caused because people simply don't know what they are doing or are physically incapable of performing the work. The remedy – or, better still, the preventative action – for lack of skill or knowledge is proper training and supervision. For aptitude and physical ability it involves making sure that the right person is chosen to do the work. For example, it makes obvious sense not to ask seafarers who are afraid of heights to work aloft.

> ### Acceptance of unsafe conditions

There are two problems here. Those seafarers who have been on board for some time may become complacent and simply stop noticing that standards have slipped. And new crew members may be reluctant to speak up about practices they are not comfortable about and, if they do, may simply accept the reply that *'this is how it is on this ship'*.

> ### Experience, assumptions and a false sense of security

Experience can trap people into making false assumptions. Two pieces of equipment may appear to be identical, but there may be important, and potentially dangerous, differences between them. Individuals should always question the assumptions they might make by asking, for example, *'do the brakes on this crane work as well as those on the one I was operating yesterday?'*.

➤ **'Rules are there to be broken'**

Some people are irritated by rules, regulations and procedures. This is particularly common when no-one has made sure that they understand why these restrictions are necessary.

It might seem that this contradicts the point about responsibility and control under 'basic motivation' above, but note that what it says there is 'an appropriate measure of control'. It is very important from the point of view both of performance and of safety for individuals to be clear about what decisions they can and cannot take.

➤ **Poor communication**

Even when people get the right information, they sometimes draw the wrong conclusions from it. Safety comes from dialogue, so that everyone understands what is to be done and why.

➤ **Stress and fatigue**

When we are tired or under pressure we make mistakes. The sinking of The Herald of Free Enterprise because the bow doors to the car deck were not shut when the ship sailed is a classic example of what can happen when individuals are exhausted and a crew is put under unreasonable operational pressure.

APPENDICES

RELEVANT IMO, ILO AND EU REGULATIONS

- The ISM Code, Chapters 1 - 13 (with items of particular relevance to safety and health on board highlighted in bold).

- The STCW Convention and its relationship to the ISM Code.

- ILO Minimum Standards Convention no. 147 (Enforced by global Port State Control).

- ILO Convention 178 concerning the inspection of seafarers working and living conditions (excerpts)

- Brief summaries and excerpts from relevant EU Council Directives for ships flying EU flags.

THE STRUCTURE OF THE ISM CODE

International Safety Management (ISM) Code means the International Management Code for the Safe Operation of Ships and Pollution Prevention as adopted by SOLAS, resolution A 741(18).

The most recent version of the Code, in force from July 2002, is reproduced in full below. We have highlighted in bold items which are particularly relevant to safety and health on board.

Note in particular:

The Code's objectives (Ch. 1.2.1):

The objectives of the Code are to ensure safety at sea, prevention of human injury or loss of life, and avoidance of damage of the environment, in particular to the marine environment, and to property.

Company's Safety Management objectives (Ch. 1.2.2):

1. Provide for safe practices in ship operation and safe working environment.

2. Establish safeguards against all identified risks.

3. Continuously improve safety management skills of personnel ashore and onboard ships, including preparing for emergencies related to both safety and environmental protection.

The SMS – Safety Management System - shall ensure (Ch. 1.2.3):

1. Compliance with mandatory rules and regulations.

2. That applicable codes, guidelines and standards recommended by IMO, Administrations (of the Flag State), classification societies and marine industry organisations are taken into account.

The Preamble

This is an important and often neglected part of the ISM Code. The preamble is crucial to understanding the Code.

Certification – Validity and Verification

Certificates granted to companies (Documents of Compliance – DOCs) and to their ships (Safety Management Certificates – SMCs) under ISM are valid for five years. In addition, proper functioning of the Code's provisions must be periodically verified. For companies, this involves an annual audit within 3 months of the date of issuing the DOC. For each ship there must be one intermediate audit within the 5 year period and this must take place between the second and third year. Further details are in the IMO Resolution A.788 (19) 'Guidelines for the Implementation of the ISM Code by Administrations'.

Chapters 14 - 16, which are not included here, cover technical details about interim certification, verification and the forms of certificates.

THE ISM CODE

(Sections with relevance to safety and health at work onboard are in **bold**)

Preamble

1. The purpose of the Code is to provide an international standard for the safe management and operation of ships and for pollution prevention.

2. The Assembly also adopted resolution A.443 (XI) by which it invited all Governments to take the necessary steps to safeguard the shipmaster in the proper discharge of his responsibilities with regard to maritime safety and the protection of the marine environment.

3. The assembly also adopted resolution A.680 (17) by which it further recognized the need for appropriate organization of management to enable it to respond to the need of those on board ships to achieve and maintain high standards of safety and environmental protection.

4. Recognizing that no two shipping companies or shipowners are the same, and that ships operate under a wide range of different conditions, the Code is based on general principles and objectives.

5. The Code is expressed in broad terms so that it can have a widespread application. Clearly, different levels of management, whether shore-based or at sea, will require varying levels of knowledge and awareness of the items outlined.

6. **The cornerstone of good safety management is commitment from the top. In matters of safety and pollution prevention it is the commitment, competence and motivation of individuals at all levels that determines the result.**

1. GENERAL

1.1 DEFINITIONS

1.1.1. *International Safety Management (ISM) Code* means the International Management Code for the Safe Operation of Ships and for Pollution Prevention as adopted by the Assembly, as may be amended by the organization.

1.1.2. *Company* means the owner of the ship or any other organisation or person such as the manager, or the bareboat charterer, who has assumed the responsibility for operation of the ship from the shipowner and who on assuming such responsibility has agreed to take over all the duties and responsibility imposed by the Code.

1.1.3. *Administration* means the Government of the State whose flag the ship is entitled to.

1.2 OBJECTIVES

1.2.1. The objectives of the Code are to ensure safety at sea, prevention of human injury or loss of life, and avoidance of damage to environment, in particular to the marine environment, and to property.

1.2.2. Safety management objectives of the Company should, inter alia:

1. provide for safe practices in ship operation and a safe working environment,

2. establish safeguards against all identified risks, and

3. continuously improve safety management skills of personnel ashore and aboard ships, including preparing for emergencies related both to safety and environmental protection.

1.2.3. The safety and management system should ensure:

1. compliance with mandatory rules and regulations; and

2. that applicable codes, guidelines and standards recommended by the Organisation, Administrations, classification societies and maritime industry organisations are taken into account.

1.2.3.1 Application

The requirements of this Code may be applied to all ships.

1.2.3.2 Functional requirements for a Safety Management System (SMS)

Every Company should develop, implement and maintain a safety management system (SMS) which includes the following functional requirements:

1. a safety and environmental protection policy;

2. instructions and procedures to ensure safe operation of ships and protection of the environment in compliance with relevant international and flag State legislation:

3. defined levels of authority and lines of communication between, and amongst, shore and shipboard personnel;

4. procedures for reporting accidents and non-conformities with the provision of this Code;

5. procedures to prepare for and respond to emergency situations;

6. procedures for internal audits and management reviews.

2. SAFETY AND ENVIRONMENTAL PROTECTION POLICY

2.1. The Company should establish a safety and environmental protection policy which describes how the objectives, given in paragraph 1.2 will be achieved.

2.2. The Company should ensure that the policy is implemented and maintained at all levels of the organisation, both ship based as well as shore based.

3. COMPANY RESPONSIBILITIES AND AUTHORITY

3.1. If the entity who is responsible for the operation of the ship is other than the owner, the owner must report the full name and details of such entity to the Administration.

3.2. **The Company should define and document the responsibility, authority and interrelations of all personnel who manage, perform and verify work relating to and affecting safety and pollution prevention.**

3.3. The Company is responsible for ensuring that adequate resources and shore based support are provided to enable the designated person to carry out their functions.

4. DESIGNATED PERSON(S)

To ensure the safe operation of each ship and to provide a link between the company and those onboard, every company, as appropriate, should designate a person or persons ashore having direct access to the highest level of management. The responsibility and authority of the designated person or persons should include monitoring the safety and pollution prevention aspects of the operation of each ship and to ensure that adequate resources and shore based support are applied, as required.

5. MASTER'S RESPONSIBILITY AND AUTHORITY

5.1. The Company should clearly define and document the master's responsibility with regard to:

1. implementing the safety and environmental protection policy of the Company;

2. motivating the crew in the observation of that policy;

3. issuing appropriate orders and instructions in a clear and simple manner;

4. verifying that specific requirements are observed; and

5. reviewing the SMS and reporting its deficiencies to the shore based management.

5.2. The Company should ensure that the SMS operating onboard the ship contains a clear statement emphasising the Masters authority. The Company should establish in the SMS that the Master has the overriding authority and the responsibility to make decisions with respect to safety and pollution prevention and to request the Company's assistance as may be necessary.

6. RESOURCES AND PERSONNEL

6.1. The Company should ensure the Master is:

1. properly qualified for command

2. fully conversant with the Company's SMS, and

3. given the necessary support so that the Master's duties can be safely performed.

6.2. The Company should ensure that each ship is manned with qualified, certified and medically fit seafarers in accordance with national and international regulations.

6.3. The Company should establish procedures to ensure that new personnel and personnel transferred to new assignments related to safety and protection of the environment are given proper familiarisation with their duties. Instructions which are essential to be provided prior to sailing should be identified, documented and given.

6.4. The Company should ensure that all personnel involved in the Company's SMS have an adequate understanding of relevant rules, regulations, codes and guidelines.

6.5. The Company should establish and maintain procedures for identifying any training which may be required in support of the SMS and ensure that such training is provided for all personnel concerned.

6.6. The Company should establish procedures by which the ship's personnel receive relevant information on the SMS in a working language or languages understood by them.

6.7. The Company should ensure that the ship's personnel are able to communicate effectively in the execution of their duties related to the SMS.

7. DEVELOPMENT OF PLANS FOR SHIPBOARD OPERATIONS

The Company should establish procedures for the preparation of plans and instructions, including checklists as appropriate, for key operations concerning the safety of the ship and the prevention of pollution. The various tasks involved should be defined and assigned to qualified personnel.

8. EMERGENCY PREPAREDNESS

8.1. The Company should establish procedures to identify, describe and respond to potential emergency shipboard situations.

8.2. The company should establish programmes for drills and exercises to prepare for emergency actions.

8.3. The SMS should provide for measures ensuring that the Company's organisation can respond at any time to hazards, accidents and emergency situations involving its ships.

9. REPORTS AND ANALYSIS OF NON-CONFORMITIES ACCIDENTS AND HAZARDOUS OCCURRENCES

9.1. The SMS should include procedures ensuring that non-conformities, accidents and hazardous situations are reported to the Company, investigated and analysed with the objective of improving safety and pollution prevention.

9.2. The Company should establish procedures for the implementation of corrective actions.

10. MAINTENANCE OF THE SHIP AND EQUIPMENT

10.1. The Company should establish procedures to ensure that the ship is maintained in conformity with the provisions of the relevant rules and regulations and with any additional requirements which may be established by the Company.

10.2. In meeting these requirements the Company should ensure that:

1. inspections are held at appropriate intervals

2. and any non-conformity is reported with is possible cause, if known

3. appropriate action is taken

4. records of these activities are maintained

10.3. The Company should establish procedures in SMS to identify equipment and technical systems the sudden operational failure of which may result in hazardous situations. The SMS should provide for specific measures aimed at promoting the reliability of such equipment or system. These measures should include the regular testing of stand-by arrangements and equipment or technical systems that are not in continuous use.

10.4. The inspections mentioned in 10.2 as well as the measures referred to in 10.3 should be integrated into the ship's operational maintenance routine.

11. DOCUMENTATION

11.1. The Company should establish and maintain procedures to control all documents and data which are relevant to the SMS.

11.2. The Company should ensure that:

1. Valid documents are available at all relevant locations

2. Changes to documents are reviewed and approved by authorised personnel

3. Obsolete documents are promptly removed.

11.3. The document used to describe and implement the SMS may be referred to as the 'Safety Management manual'. Documentation should be kept in a form that the Company considers most effective. Each ship should carry on board all documentation relevant to that ship.

12. COMPANY VERIFICATION, REVIEW AND EVALUATION

12.1. The Company should carry out internal safety audits to verify whether safety and pollution activities comply with the SMS.

12.2. The Company should periodically evaluate the efficiency and when needed review the SMS in accordance with procedures established by the Company.

12.3. Personnel carrying out audits should be independent of the areas being audited unless this is impracticable due to the size and nature of the Company.

12.4. Personnel carrying out audits should be independent of the areas being audited unless this is impracticable due to the size and nature of the Company.

12.5. The results of the audits and reviews should be brought to the attention of all personnel having responsibility in the area involved.

12.6. The management personnel responsible for the area involved should take timely corrective action on deficiencies found.

13. CERTIFICATION, VERIFICATION AND CONTROL

13.1. The ship should be operated by a Company which is issued a document of compliance relevant to that ship.

13.2. A document of compliance should be issued for every Company complying with the requirements of the ISM Code by the Administration, by an organisation recognised by the organisation, or by the Government of the country, acting on behalf of the Administration in which the Company has chosen to conduct its business. This document should be accepted as evidence that the Company is capable of complying with the requirements of the Code.

13.3. Copy of such document should be placed on board on order that the Master, if so asked, may produce it for the verification of the Administration or organisations recognised by it.

13.4. A certificate, called a Safety Management Certificate, should be issued to a ship by the Administration or organisation recognised by the Administration. The Administration should, when issuing the certificate, verify that the Company and its shipboard management operate in accordance with the approved SMS.

13.5. The Administration or an organisation recognised by the Administration should periodically verify the proper functioning of the ship's SMS as approved.

THE STCW CONVENTION AND ITS RELATIONSHIP TO THE ISM CODE

In parallel with the implementation of the ISM Code, the shipping industry is also faced with the enforcement of the STCW 95 Convention for 'Seafarers Training, Certification and Watch-keeping'. This is an amendment of the earlier STCW-78 Convention.

The STCW Code and Convention is too extensive to be quoted in full here. We have therefore confined ourselves to a short excerpt of the most relevant items. We have also shown how, with respect to the health and safety work onboard, STCW 95 relates to the STCW-78 Convention and the ISM Code.

The STCW Convention for Seafarers Training, Certification and Watchkeeping

Improvements

The STCW 95 Convention contains the following amendments and improvements:

1. Crew training and certification will be internationally unified, and where necessary upgraded, in a global scheme.

2. The seafarers vocational training syllabus will be more specific and standardised.

3. Seafarers are now obliged to be medically examined by approved and authorised doctors.

4. Seafarers are guaranteed familiarisation training, covering both routine and emergency duties, when they arrive onboard. This training must be conducted by an approved, competent person.

5. There are specified rest periods for seafarers (a minimum of 10 hours per day) to avoid fatigue.

6. Ships must have readily accessible documentation and data for all seafarers employed onboard, including certificates and qualification documents, and records of experience, training, medical fitness and competence in assigned duties.

7. There are clear requirements laid down for shipping companies covering training and approval of Company personnel for the evaluation, training and continuous assessment of crews.

8. There are clear requirements for Administrations to ensure that companies comply with their obligations for evaluation, training and assessment of crews.

9. There are clear requirements for Administrations to provide adequate control of institutions involved in crew training and certification.

Implementation

The basic steps for STCW-95 Convention were as follows:

1. **1st February 1997:** The official implementation date. The amendments to the Convention were officially adopted, but Administrations could still allow education, training and certification in accordance with STCW-78.

2. **1st August 1998:** After this date Administrations were obliged to have approved educational programmes, training courses and evaluation of new candidates.

   But Administrations may still allow Education, Training and Certification of seafarers who have already commenced their maritime education in accordance with STCW-78.

3. **1st February 2002:** After this date all transitional measures came to an end and all requirements of the amended STCW Convention must have been implemented.

STCW and the ISM Code

There was some confusion during the transitional period leading to full implementation of STCW 95. Certain required provisions of the ISM Code which also formed part of STCW 95 came into effect before STCW-95 was fully implemented.

The table below will help clarify the relationship and practical implications for shipping companies between STCW 95 and provisions in the ISM Code:

STCW REQUIREMENT	ISM CODE REQUIREMENT
In general: A Safe Manning certificate is required, issued by the Flag State (SOLAS), with reference to IMO Resolution A.481 (XII).	
	Ch. 2 Safety and Environment Policy
1. Training Policy required	Check the Policy statement in SMS
2. Shipboard Familiarisation	Check Policy statement and shipboard SMS
3. Fitness for duty	Check Policy statement in SMS
	Check national requirements for medical fitness
	Check national requirements for hours of rest
	Ch. 3. Company Responsibility and Authority
4. In-service training: – Has the company's training supervisor, training officer and assessor been defined, documented and assigned?	Applies only when a company performs such in-service training, or to seafarers starting their training/education after 1 August 1998.
	Ch. 5. Masters Responsibility and Authority
5. In-service training: – Has the Master's responsibility for training been defined/documented?	As 4 above.
	Ch. 6 Resources and Personnel
6. Familiarisation. – Procedures in place for crew members and other personnel for familiarisation with ship and duties before being assigned? – Is the task of familiarisation assigned to knowledgeable crew members onboard?	– Check Company's SMS for familiarisation procedures, execution and records. Ensure that sufficient time have been allowed, and the proper language have been understood. Verify the outcome by asking questions relevant to procedures and arrangements.
7. Knowledge of maritime legislation. – Do the Company ensure that officers have sufficient knowledge of pertinent legislation?	– Check that relevant personnel are aware of relevant international and national legislation currently applicable. – Check that relevant personnel have knowledge of regulations pertinent to their duties, and that they are able to refer to or find those regulations

STCW REQUIREMENT	ISM CODE REQUIREMENT
8. Fitness for duty. – Does the Company keep records of work hours and rest hours?	Refer to records of work and rest hours (Most Flag States have national legislation)
9. Has the Company put in place safeguards against drug and alcohol abuse?	Refer to alcohol and drug abuse policy
10. Have the Company routines for training, updating or replacement of the individual crew members?	"Updating" to be included (for present position).

11. In-service training.
  – Is training conducted according to an approved training programme?
  – Is training registered in an approved record book ?
	As 4 above.

12. Special training for tankers.
Are training programmes applied as required for:
  – Oil tankers
  – Chemical tankers
  – Liquefied gas tankers.
	Verification by course diplomas or other similar means of evidence.

13. Special training for:
  – Ro-Ro passenger ships
  – Passenger ships.
  – Passenger safety
  – Cargo safety
  – Hull integrity
  – Crisis Management
  – Human Behaviour
  – (as req. by Flag State)
	Check relevant procedures, documentary evidence or similar to make sure that required training has been carried out. Training in crisis management and human behaviour may be required under national legislation.

14. Common language. – Has the Company decided common language for this particular crew ?	Check SMS procedures for ensuring a common language, and that a common language has been decided. (Auditors may check by asking several crew members what language they use when carrying out their duties.)
15. Communication – Designated crew members (as navigating officers) shall have a sufficient knowledge of English	Check that relevant procedures are in place. Also any pending national legislation
	Ch. 7. Plans for shipboard Operations
16. Crew co-ordination. – Are there procedures in place to ensure crew co-ordination in performing functions vital to safety or pollution prevention?	Check that activities vital to safety and pollution prevention are in place, and that there is documentary evidence that drills and other exercises have been done. Crew co-ordination may be verified by questions related to particularly relevant operations, such as bunker operations, lifeboat launching, fire-fighting, etc.

STCW REQUIREMENT	ISM CODE REQUIREMENT
	Ch. 8. Emergency Preparedness
17. Crew co-ordination – Are there necessary programs for drills and exercises to prepare for emergency actions?	Some Administrations may require demonstrations of lifeboat drills during ISM Code shipboard auditing.
	Ch. 11. Documentation Control
18. Seafarers documentation – Are documents and data relevant to all seafarers maintained and readily accessible onboard?	Originals of certificates and other relevant crew documentation shall be kept in onboard.
19. Seafarers' certificates – Are all certificates and documentation of competence required by STCW-95 verified for authenticity and validity?	Check SMS procedures for this, and also that procedures have been carried out. (In addition Administrations issuing the certificates are required to maintain records and provide information upon request.)

NOTE:

Even with the strictest implementation of both the ISM Code and the STCW Convention, the final goal of crews consisting entirely of fully qualified professional seafarers cannot be accomplished by maritime academies ashore and the provision of procedures and instructions onboard only. The seafarer's profession is like any other. Skill, knowledge and procedures are essential, but on their own they are not enough. High quality standards for less experienced seafarers must also be derived from observation of practical examples set by their more experienced colleagues.

This is a working principle to be found in the best run organisations, both ashore and at sea.

ILO MINIMUM STANDARDS CONVENTION NO. 147

(Enforced by global Port State Control)

The General Conference of the International Labour Organization, ... having decided upon the adoption of certain proposals with regard to substandard vessels, particularly those registered under flags of convenience, ... adopts ... the following Convention:

Article 1

1. Except otherwise provided in this Article, this Convention applies to every seagoing ship, whether publicly or privately owned, which is engaged in the transport of cargo or passengers for the purpose of trade or is employed for any other commercial purpose.

2. National laws or regulation shall determine when ships are to be regarded as seagoing ships for the purpose of this convention.

3. This Convention applies to seagoing tugs.

Article 2

Each member which ratifies this Convention undertakes-

(a) to have laws or regulations laying down, for ships registered in its territory:

    (i)   safety standards, including standards of competency, hours of work and manning, so as to ensure the safety of life on board ship;

    (ii)   appropriate social security measures, and

    (iii)   shipboard conditions of employment and shipboard living arrangements, in so far as these, in the opinion of the Member, are not covered by collective agreements or laid down by competent courts in a manner equally binding on the shipowners and seafarers concerned; and to satisfy that the provisions of such laws and regulations are substantially equivalent to the Conventions or Articles of Conventions referred to in the Appendix to this Convention, in so far as the Member is not otherwise bound to give effect to the Conventions in question.

(b) to exercise effective jurisdiction or control over ships which are registered in its territory in respect of:

    (i)   safety standards, including standards of competency, hours of work and manning, prescribed by national laws or regulations

    (ii)   social security measures prescribed by national laws or regulations;

    (iii)   shipboard conditions of employment and shipboard living arrangements prescribed by national laws or regulations, or laid down by competent courts in a manner equally binding on the shipowners and seafarers concerned;

(c) to satisfy itself that measures for the effective control of other shipboard conditions of employment and living arrangements, where it has no effective jurisdiction, are agreed between shipowners or their organisations and seafarers' organisation constituted in accordance with the substantive provisions of the Freedom of Association and Protection of the Right to Organise Convention, 1948, and the Right to Organise and Collective Bargaining Convention, 1949;

(d) to ensure that:

    (i)   adequate procedures – subject to overall supervision by competent authority, after tripartite consultation amongst that authority and the representative organisations of shipowners and seafarers where appropriate exist for the engagement of seafarers on ships registered in its territory and for the investigation of complaints arising in that connection;

(ii)   adequate procedures – subject to overall supervision by the competent authority, after tripartite consultation amongst that authority and the representative organisation of shipowners and seafarers where appropriate - exist for the investigation of any complaint made in connection with and, if possible, at the time of the engagement in its territory of seafarers of its own nationality on ships registered in a foreign country, and that such complaint as well as any complaint made in connection with and, if possible, at the time of the engagement in its territory of foreign seafarers on ships registered in a foreign country, is promptly reported by its competent authority to the competent authority of the country in which the ship is registered, with a copy to the Director General of the International Labour Office;

(e) to ensure that seafarers employed on ships registered in its territory are properly qualified or trained for the duties for which they are engaged, due regard being had to the Vocational Training (Seafarers) Recommendation, 1970;

(f) to verify by inspection or other appropriate means that ships registered in its territory comply with applicable international labour Conventions in force which it has ratified, with the laws and regulations required by subparagraph (a) of this Article, as may be appropriate under national law, with applicable collective agreements;

(g) to hold an official inquiry into any serious casualty involving ships registered in its territory, particularly those involving injury and/or loss of life, the final report of such inquiry normally to be made public.

Article 3

Any member which has ratified this convention shall, as far as practicable, advise its nationals on the possible problems of signing on a ship registered in a State which has not ratified the Convention, until it is satisfied that the standards equivalent to those fixed by this Convention are being applied. Measures taken by the ratifying State to this effect shall not be in contradiction with the principle of free movement of workers stipulated by treaties to which the two States concerned may be parties.

Article 4

1. If a member which has ratified the Convention and in whose port a ship calls in normal course of its business or for operational reasons receives a complaint or obtains evidence that that the ship does not conform the standards of this Convention, after it has come into force, it may prepare a report addressed to the government of the country in which the ship is registered, with a copy to the Director General of the International Labour Office, and may take measures necessary to rectify any conditions on board which are clearly hazardous to safety or health.

2. In taking such measures, the Member shall forthwith notify the nearest maritime, consular or diplomatic representative of the flag State and shall, if possible, have such representative present. It shall not unreasonably detain or delay the ship.

3. For the purpose of this Article, 'complaint' means information submitted by a member of the crew, a professional body, an association, a trade union or generally, any person with an interest in the safety of the ship, including an interest in safety or health hazards to its crew.

Article 5

1. This Convention is open to the ratification of members which:

   (a) are parties to the international Convention for the Safety of Life at Sea, 1960, or any of the international Convention for the Safety of Life at Sea, 1974, or any Convention subsequently revising these Conventions; and

   (b) are parties to the International Convention on Load Lines, 1966, or any Convention subsequently revising that Convention: and

   (c) are parties to, or have implemented the provisions of, the Regulations for Preventing Collisions at Sea of 1960, or the Convention on the International Regulations for Preventing Collisions at Sea, 1972, or any Convention subsequently revising these international instruments.

2. This Convention is further open to the ratification of any member which, on ratification, undertakes to fulfil the requirements to which ratification is made subject to paragraph 1 of this Article and which are not yet ratified.

3. The formal ratification of this Convention shall be communicated to the Director-General of the International Labour Office for registration.

Article 6

1. This Convention shall be binding only upon those members of the International Labour Organisation whose ratifications have been registered with the Director General.

2. It shall come into force twelve months after the date on which there have been registered ratifications by at least ten Members with a total share in the world shipping gross tonnage of 25 per cent.

3. Thereafter, this Convention shall come into force for any member twelve months after the date on which its ratifications have been registered.

Appendix

Minimum Age Convention, 1973 (No. 138), ...

Shipowners' Liability (Sick and Injured Seaman) Convention, 1936 (No. 55), ...

Medical Examinations (Seafarers) Convention, 1946 (No. 73), ...

Prevention of Accidents (Seafarers) Convention, 1970 (No. 134) (Articles 4 and 7)

Accommodation of Crews Convention (Revised), 1949 (No. 92)

Food and Catering (Ships Crew) Convention, 1946 (No. 68) (Article 5)

Officers Competency Certificates Convention, 1936, (No. 53) (Articles 3 and 4)

Seamen's Articles of Agreement Convention, 1926 (No. 22)

Repatriation of Seamen Convention, 1926 (No. 23)

Freedom of Association and Protection of the Right to Organise Convention, 1948 (No. 87)

Right to Organise and Collective Bargaining Convention, 1949 (No. 98).

ILO CONVENTION 178 CONCERNING THE INSPECTION OF SEAFARERS WORKING AND LIVING CONDITIONS (EXCERPTS)

Part I. Scope and definitions

Article I

1. Except as otherwise provided in this Article, this Convention applies to every seagoing ship, whether publicly or privately owned, which is registered in the territory of a Member for which the Convention is in force and is engaged in the transport of cargo or passengers for the purpose of trade or is employed for any other commercial purpose. ...

2. For the purpose of this Convention:

   e. the term "seafarers working and living conditions" means the condition such as those related to the standards of maintenance and cleanliness of shipboard living and working areas, minimum age, articles of agreement, food and catering, crew accommodation, recruitment, manning, qualifications, hours of work, medical examinations, prevention of occupational accidents, medical care, sickness and injury benefits, social welfare and related matters, repatriation, terms and conditions of employment which are subject to national laws and regulations, and freedom of association as defined in the Freedom of Association and Protection of the right to Organise Convention, 1948, of the International Labour Organisation.

Part II. Organization of inspection

Article 2

1. Each Member for which the Convention is in force shall maintain a system of inspection of 'seafarers working and living conditions'.

Article 3

1. Each Member shall ensure that all ships registered in its territory are inspected at intervals not exceeding three years and when practicable, annually, to verify that the 'seafarers working and living conditions' on board conform to national laws and regulations.

2. If a Member receives a complaint or obtains evidence that a ship registered in its territory does not conform to national laws and regulations of 'seafarers working and living conditions', the Member shall take measures to inspect the ship as soon as possible.

3. In cases of substantial changes in construction or accommodation arrangements, the ship shall be inspected within three months of such changes.

Article 4.

Each Member shall appoint inspectors qualified for the performance of their duties and shall take the necessary steps to satisfy itself that inspectors are available in sufficient number to meet the requirements of this Convention.

OVERVIEW OF THE 4 MAIN EU COUNCIL DIRECTIVES FOR SAFETY AND HEALTH AT WORK. THESE APPLY TO SHIPS FLYING THE FLAG OF EU MEMBER STATES

THE MAIN FRAMEWORK DIRECTIVE

1. **Council Directive 89/391: "The introduction of measures to encourage improvements in the safety and health of workers"**

General provisions:

- The employer must ensure that an assessment is made of the risks affecting safety and health at work.

- The employer must ensure that the workers of their undertaking receive information on among other things, the safety and health risks, preventive measures, first aid, fire fighting, risk assessments, etc.

- The employers must consult workers and/or their representatives on matters concerning their safety and health.

- The employer must ensure that each worker receives adequate and job specific safety and health training.

- Each worker has an obligation to take care of his/her own safety and health and to make correct use of machinery, dangerous substances, personal protective equipment, etc.

INDIVIDUAL DIRECTIVES

2. **Council Directive 89/655: "Use of work equipment"**

Main points:

- The employer must base the choice of work equipment on the specific working conditions and hazards existing for workers in order to eliminate or minimise those hazards. Where it is not possible to use work equipment which does not jeopardise the health and safety of workers, the employer must minimise the risks.

- Adequate instructions and training in the use of work equipment must be provided for the workers by the employer.

- Use, maintenance or repair of work equipment involving a specific risk may only be carried out by workers specifically qualified for the task.

3. **Council Directive 89/656: "Use of personal protective equipment"**

Main points:

- The use of personal protective equipment is required when risks cannot be avoided or limited by technical means or methods or procedures of work organisation.

- Personal protective equipment must comply with the relevant community provisions on designs and manufacture.

- All personal protective equipment must be appropriate for the risks involved, without leading to any increased risk. It must correspond to the existing conditions at the workplace and must fit the wearer correctly.

- The employer must provide the personal protective equipment and pay any expense in connection therewith and must ensure that it is in good working order and hygienic condition.

- Training and the organisation of demonstrations in the wearing of the personal protective equipment also lie with the employer.

4. **Council Directive 90/269: "Manual handling of loads"**

Main points:

- The employer must try to avoid the need for manual handling of loads by workers. He must therefore take appropriate organisational measures or make use of, for instance, mechanical equipment. Where manual handling cannot be avoided, the employer must try to reduce the risk involved.

- It is also the employer's duty to inform the workers of the weight of the load to be carried, the centre of gravity of the heaviest side of the load and the risk of incorrect handling.

EU Standards for "Health and Safety work in the workplace" (EU Commission's Article 118A)

FEATURES OF THE EU STANDARD FOR HEALTH AND SAFETY AT WORK

The EU's Treaty of Rome Harmonisation Clause, Article.100A, deals with special regulations for member states. The EU standards are guidelines, but the long term intention is to establish an EU standard system which is ratified for all member states.

This means that, while individual member states have the freedom to create national regulations and requirements which do not comply with the EU standards, they must be able to demonstrate to the Commission that any differences are justified. Member states whose national legislation complies with the EU standard are naturally not subject to this requirement.

FEATURES OF THE EU STANDARD RELATED TO HEALTH AND SAFETY TRAINING

➤ They require more active participation from companies.

➤ They require companies to provide qualified safety and health personnel to establish a more active co-operation between companies and their ships.

➤ They expect training of safety and health personnel to be focussed on the particular requirements of the workplace (the ship), and the outcomes of training to be verified.

➤ They require companies to carry out risk assessments for their ships.

➤ They expect the management, follow-up and verification of safety and health on board to be dynamic and continuous, both in general, and in particular after any significant change in personnel, equipment or operating conditions.

➤ Companies are required to assess and evaluate satisfactory training methods.

INDEX